PRAYER

Catholic Spirituality for Adults

General Editor:
Michael Leach

Other Books in the Series
Reconciliation

PRAYER

❊

Joyce Rupp

ORBIS BOOKS
Maryknoll, New York 10545

Founded in 1970, Orbis Books endeavors to publish works that enlighten the mind, nourish the spirit, and challenge the conscience. The publishing arm of the Maryknoll Fathers and Brothers, Orbis seeks to explore the global dimensions of the Christian faith and mission, to invite dialogue with diverse cultures and religious traditions, and to serve the cause of reconciliation and peace. The books published reflect the views of their authors and do not represent the official position of the Maryknoll Society. To learn more about Maryknoll and Orbis Books, please visit our website at www.maryknoll.org.

Grateful acknowledgment is given for permission to reprint from "To Live with the Spirit" in *The House at Rest,* by Jessica Powers, 1984, published by Carmelite Monastery. All copyrights, Carmelite Monastery, Pewaukee, WI. Used with permission.

Queries regarding rights and permissions should be addressed to:
Orbis Books, P.O. Box 308, Maryknoll, NY 10545-0308.

Manufactured in the United States of America.

Library of Congress Cataloging-in-Publication Data
Rupp, Joyce.
    Prayer / Joyce Rupp.
      p. cm.
    ISBN 978-1-57075-712-9
    1. Prayer – Biblical teaching. 2. Prayer – Christianity. 3. Spiritual life – Catholic Church. I. Title.
BS680.P64R87 2007
248.3′2 – dc22

                                       2007005787

Contents

Introduction to
Catholic Spirituality for Adults

C ATHOLIC SPIRITUALITY FOR ADULTS explores the deepest dimension of spirituality, that place in the soul where
faith meets understanding. When we reach that place we
begin to see as if for the first time. We are like the blind man in
the Gospel who could not believe his eyes: "And now I see!"

Catholicism is about seeing the good of God that is in front
of our eyes, within us, and all around us. It is about learning
to see Christ Jesus with the eyes of Christ Jesus, the Way, the
Truth, and the Life.

Only when we *see* who we are as brothers and sisters of
Christ and children of God can we begin to *be* like Jesus and
walk in his Way. "As you think in your heart, so you are"
(Prov. 23:7).

Catholic Spirituality for Adults is for those of us who want
to make real, here and now, the words we too once learned.
It is designed to help us go beyond information to transformation. "When I was a child; I spoke as a child, I understood
as a child, I thought as a child; but when I became an adult,
I put away childish things" (1 Cor. 13:11).

The contributors to the series are the best Catholic authors
writing today. We have asked them to explore the deepest

dimension of their own faith and to share with us what they are learning to see. Topics covered range from prayer — "Be still and know that I am God" (Ps. 46:10) — to our purpose in life — coming to know "that God has given us eternal life, and that this life is in his Son" (1 John 5:11) — to simply getting through the day — "Put on compassion, kindness, humility, and love" (Col. 3:12).

Each book in this series reflects Christ's active and loving presence in the world. The authors celebrate our membership in the mystical body of Christ, help us to understand our spiritual unity with the entire family of God, and encourage us to express Christ's mission of love, peace, and reconciliation in our daily lives.

Catholic Spirituality for Adults is the fruit of a publishing partnership between Orbis Books, the publishing arm of the Catholic Foreign Mission Society of America (Maryknoll), and RCL Benziger, a leading provider of religious and family life education for all ages. This series is rooted in vital Catholic traditions and committed to a continuing standard of excellence.

Michael Leach
General Editor

Author's Introduction

EVER SINCE my enthusiastic second-grade teacher inspired me by talking about Jesus as her lifelong companion, I have yearned for and actively sought a relationship with
God. Because of her passionate teaching, a vast hunger for the
Other opened up in me. This quest has never ended. I know
my journey is not unique in this regard. Other people have
similar longings. They, too, seek a treasured and true friendship with God, a closeness requiring constant faithfulness to
prayer.

When publisher Michael Leach asked me to consider writing a book on prayer, I hesitated. My first thought was:
"There must be ten thousand books already written on this
topic. Why would I write another one?" Then I recalled how
I continually read book after book related to spiritual growth
even though I feel at home with God most of the time. Why
do I, and many others, want to learn more about prayer?
Is it because our human effort to maintain contact with the
Holy One is vague and intangible? Could it be the result of
acquiring a taste for the divine and yearning for ever more of
this precious gift? Do books about prayer continue to claim
our attention because we can never get our arms completely
around or totally claim an embrace of the Holy? Do we want

to learn more about prayer because we seek an affirmation of our spiritual journey, some surety that we are "doing prayer right"?

I suspect the answer lies somewhere beneath and beyond each of these questions. Our yearning for God is never fully satisfied. And we are never really sure we are praying in a way that is best for our spiritual growth. Some part of our self nags at us from time to time, causing us to wonder if we truly know how to pray, and if our prayer has any worth and effect. I do believe that most of us long for some evidence that our God-relationship is real and true. Even though the life and message of Jesus revealed the Holy One to us, we still falter and sputter on our way into daily relationship with this divine being. Because there is endless mystery to our inner journey with God, we can't help but find a bit of ambiguity seeping around the edges. One week we are happy and comfortable with prayer. The next, we are restless and uncertain.

About the time we settle in and feel satisfied with our prayer, life upends us with some unexpected event or internal rumbling, and we find ourselves wondering how best to pray amid the circumstances. Faith is absolutely necessary because we cannot prove much about prayer. We can attest to the value of staying in touch with God, but we cannot verify how this happens with absolute certainty.

Thomas Merton referred to this uncertainty when he prayed about his inner life. Even though Merton was a Trappist monk who prayed faithfully each day, he admitted he did not know for sure where he was going on his journey with God. In spite of this unknowing, Merton expressed faith-filled confidence that God was not only with him, but also knew and accepted the desire of his heart:

> But I believe that the desire to please you does in fact please you. And I hope that I have that desire in all that I am doing. I hope that I will never do anything apart from that desire. And I know that if I do this, you will lead me by the right road, though I may know nothing about it. Therefore, I will trust you always though I may seem to be lost and in the shadow of death. I will not fear, for you are ever with me, and you will never leave me to face my perils alone.

The longer we pray, the more we realize prayer is bigger than we are, more expansive and deeper. When we least expect it, our prayer brings us into further clarity about who we are and how we are to be with God and the world. These experiences encourage us to lessen our stronghold on wanting to control, to know and have proof. Unexpected graced moments in prayer restore our confidence in the process and help us trust our intention to become more loving. These little glimpses encourage us to give ourselves to what we believe to be of most value. We leave the *finished product* of prayer to the One who knows the longings of our heart.

Like Merton, we trust our intention to be in a committed union with God. We give ourselves daily to the way of prayer that seems to best keep us growing into wholeness. We lean on the promises and messages we have learned from the journey of Jesus, whose life tells us that we glimpse the effectiveness of prayer by looking at how we live. Our prayer experience leads us outward into the larger world where the love growing in our hearts reaches out with Christlike compassion to embrace all of life.

What Is Prayer?

Prayer itself is ethereal, baffling, uncertain, and impossible to fully explain. On the other hand, methods and styles of prayer are specific, practical, definable, understandable, and evident.

"Prayer" means many things to many people. The framework of prayer is either *personal* (alone) or *communal* (joining with others.) The approach in both personal and communal prayer can be either "formal" (based on a structured form and wording, often designed or prepared by someone else) or "informal" (created to meet one's own individual style). I use the word "prayer" in this book to refer to *personal prayer,* both formal and informal, unless otherwise indicated.

In Christian prayer, we "pray" anytime we deliberately choose to relate to God. Thus, prayer consists of a vast assortment of modes, including: using words to converse with God, using no words with the aim of listening quietly and savoring divine presence, ruminating over thoughts and ideas, trying not to have any thoughts and ideas, extending love and receiving love, imaging and visualizing, and searching for guidance by discerning choices and decisions. Within these modes, there are numerous human expressions in communicating with God: intercessory, praise, contrition, gratitude, grieving, searching, celebrating, struggling, etc.

Varied methods comprise the content of prayer: reciting the psalms alone or with others, pondering scripture passages or other sacred texts, using repetition such as a word or phrase in centering meditation, praying the rosary, carrying on a conversation with God, walking meditatively, enjoying the beauty and wonder of nature, using the written prayers of others, journaling one's own reflections and prayer, sitting in solitude and contemplation, joining others for Eucharistic liturgy or participating in other sacramental celebrations, reading spiritually oriented books that help one pause to ponder and draw inspiration for communion with God and, every now and then, doing what my friend Judy Cauley terms "emergency prayer," which consists of just one loudly spoken word: "HELP!" These ways, plus all those unexpected moments in the midst of life when we sense a oneness with the Great Mystery, are part of what is known as "prayer."

Praying does not always take place in a contained or predetermined place of reflection. We never know when there might be an interior turning toward the One who dwells within us and among us. Going for a walk or a run, stopping at night to bless sleeping children, driving past a homeless person, looking up to see a bright star in the heavens, receiving a note from a cherished friend, turning toward a spouse in pleasurable love, reading a story in the newspaper, hearing the pain in a colleague's anguish, waiting in a check-out line — at any time and any place we can be surprised and drawn into communion by the unanticipated sense of God's nearness.

Throughout this book, I speak consistently of an immanent deity who is not far from us, who dwells within and among us, One "in whom we live and move and have our being" (Acts 17:28). This notion of immanence is vital for prayer because it grounds us in a trust of God's abiding presence. Noted theologian Karl Rahner writes:

> When I say that one can meet God immediately in your time too, just like in mine, I mean really God, the God past all grasp, the mystery beyond speech, the darkness that is light only to those who let themselves be swallowed by it unconditionally, the God who is now beyond all names. But equally it was just this God, no other, that I experienced as the God who descends to us, who comes near to us, in whose incomprehensible fire we do not in fact burn up, but rather come to be for the first time, and are eternally affirmed.

When we come to prayer, God remains elusive and beyond our control but, at the same time, is reachable and touchable. This does not deny the transcendence or "otherness" of divinity. Certainly God is much larger than any one individual. However, when we enter into personal prayer, I believe we do so in the presence of a divine being who breathes with us and is available to us in the veiled aura of godly friendship.

As I wrote this book, I looked back over my years of intentionally connecting with God and gathered what has helped me maintain a faithful practice of prayer. It is not my intention to take anyone away from a particular way of praying. Rather, my goal for this book is that it encourage each reader in his or her relationship with God, that it help each one pray in whatever way seems most suitable. Whatever your under-standing of divinity is and however you choose to pray, I hope the following chapters inspire you to nurture your inte-rior realm each day and that you will grow in cherishing your life with the Holy One. May you be led forth to be a blessing of compassion in a world crying out for loving kindness and courageous justice.

Let us be confident that our faithfulness to prayer will sus-tain our relationship with God and transform us at the core of our life.

Entering into a Relationship

When did you first
weave your way into my life,
Beloved?

When did you first
entice me
with your contagious
colors of love?

When did the mystery
of your kindness stir
so strongly
I could no longer deny your grace?

I do not know the precise moment.
Perhaps there never was one.

More, it seems to me,
are the countless times,
endless ways, you enter,
thread by thread,
the pattern of my days,

your presence inaudibly
interlacing my every moment,

your whispers and sighs,
your breathy voice
in the ear of my heart,

persuading me into your embrace.

Please, Beloved,
never stop encouraging me.

Draw me daily
into the sanctuary
of your enduring love.

—Joyce Rupp

Prayer fastens the soul to God.
—Julian of Norwich

IN EVERY AWAKENED ENCOUNTER with the Holy One, we enter the inner path where God's heart and ours meet. Among the numerous books I have read on the subject of prayer, the best description I have ever found for this spiritual practice is the one Kenneth Leech gives in *True Prayer:* "To pray is to enter into a relationship with God and to have that relationship make a difference in my life."

Establishing and developing a *relationship* is the nucleus of all Christian prayer. This bond is created with *someone,* and that *someone* is God. Our Source of Life continually bids each of us into a loving union. The process of prayer unfolds in a way similar to Jesus inviting his disciples to follow him into deeper friendship, a closeness that did not develop instantly. Prayer is a kind of companionship that develops step by step, as we are drawn into an ever expanding oneness of love.

Many years may pass before we really believe our connectedness to the Holy One is enduring and true. Even when we do believe this, cloudy times of questioning the worth and effectiveness of our relationship with God are not unusual. On the other hand, sometimes our prayer life offers us a profound consolation in which we become convinced that this relationship is solid and enduring. In these times of consolation, graced moments arise in which we are swept away with the profoundness of our communion with the divine.

"Prayer" is not only about entering into a relationship with God; it is also about *being changed*. Healthy prayer strengthens our bond with the Creator and it also transforms us. Every encounter with God provides the opportunity for us to grow spiritually. Prayer makes a difference in our life because it nudges and persuades us to develop Christlike qualities in our attitude and actions. Through prayer we become more loving, gracious, compassionate, and justice-oriented human beings. When this happens, we are altered in a positive way and the world we touch is also changed for the better.

Come and See

As in all true friendships, something stirred within the hearts of the disciples when they were with Jesus. They wanted to know him better and sought ways of doing so. John's Gospel describes how the disciples asked Jesus where he was staying. This was their indirect way of saying: "Tell us more about who you are." Jesus took them up on their inquisitive desire and invited them to spend time with him: "Come and you will see" (John 1:35–42). In our own way, when we enter into prayer, we are like the disciples, saying, "Tell us who you are. And tell us who we are in relation to you."

When we choose to pray we accept the invitation to *come and see* who this God of goodness is, and to *come and see* who we are as God's cherished one. Prayer is an essential way of kindling and developing this relationship. If we are going to have quality prayer, we will need to take time to *stay* with the Holy One in prayer, to become familiar with the depth of

Love in the center of our being. As we increasingly commit ourselves to keeping this relationship alive and thriving, not only is more of God's essence revealed; we also come to know more of our own true self.

Trusting anyone with our shadow side is difficult to do. In prayer we risk allowing our whole self to be revealed and known. As we do so, we grow in our ability to be our bare-bones-self with God. This does not happen automatically. Growth in trust requires deliberate choices to spend time with the Other, humbly opening up, believing that all of who we are will be received with merciful kindness. This relationship will not grow without intentional, quality time in which we give ourselves to God with confidence, yielding to the love of this hospitable presence.

False justifications for not praying fall away when we perceive the priceless value of our union with God. If we have time to shop, we have time to pray. If we have enough minutes to read the daily newspaper or work a crossword puzzle, we have enough minutes to pray. If we have space in our schedule to watch television or browse the Internet, we have space to pray. All the rationalizations and excuses for being unable to pray are left behind once we allow God to claim our heart.

The Mutuality of the Relationship

Long ago, during my novice year in religious community, I first experienced what it is like "to fall in love with God," to want to be united with this incredible, attractive mystery. The focus of my novitiate year was to pay close attention to the interior life, to allow silence and solitude to be the fundamental part of the year's experience. Until this significant time of my spiritual journey, I prayed regularly, but I thought of this relationship as mostly a one-way encounter. I believed everything depended on my efforts to get God's attention. I thought it was up to me to entice God to draw near. What I did not know is that God longed to gain a fuller entrance into my life.

As the days and months passed, I not only understood, I also *felt* that my longing was not one-way. Eventually, it dawned on me that God was seeking me, in fact, had already sought and persuaded me to enter into a relationship firmly founded on love. For the first time, I truly believed this to be so. My awareness of God's nearness brought me surprising consolation and comfort. The developing sense of mutuality in this love filled me with quiet joy.

This awakening helped me to finally understand the ancient words of the psalmist: "O God, you have probed me and you know me; you know when I sit and when I stand . . . with all my ways you are familiar" (Ps. 139:1–3). As prayer unfolds, we become *familiar* with God and allow God to become familiar with us. When this movement occurs, there is cause for abundant gratitude because the relationship is based on a firm foundation of trust and acceptance.

My "falling in love" with God was not a lovey-dovey feeling. Growth toward dedication and devotion more aptly describe what took place in my heart. The emotional tone of my prayer contained the strong yearning and desire expressed in Psalm 63:2, in which the psalmist parallels life without divine communion to that of a dry, parched land seeking the moisture needed for survival: "O God, you are my God whom I seek; for you my flesh pines and my soul thirsts like the earth, parched, lifeless and without water."

The German mystic Mechtild of Magdeburg depicted this acute longing for communion with God as that of a magnet being drawn to the divine. While this inner movement is dynamic and powerful, it may be marked by a quiet persistence rather than unrestrained or obvious passion. This yearning for God is sometimes indicated by an unnamable restlessness or a perpetual searching.

My developing closeness with God did not become clear until after months of struggle with daily meditation and communal prayer. I never would have considered this time in my life as a kind of *falling in love with God* until I noticed a gradual conviction settling in my soul. This confidence was due to my desire and decision to choose God above all else. Living with this conviction meant I would need to be deliberate about being in this relationship every day of my life in order to keep that choice utmost in my heart.

Similar experiences of spiritual growth are confided to me periodically by those who come for spiritual direction. I recall the time a middle-aged woman came from a week-long retreat and hesitantly described her experience with these words, "I feel embarrassed to tell you this, but I fell in love with God during these past days." Along with joy for her experience, I also felt a certain sadness about her discomfort when she spoke of her graced encounter with God. I remembered my own past reluctance to do so.

For many years I never told others about my developing relationship with the Holy One. This closeness seemed too personal and delicate to place in the open space between myself and anyone else, even a spiritual director. Once I began to reveal my deep desire for greater union with the Holy One, I was surprised that others also found courage to speak more freely about their journey of developing intimacy. I've noticed how this sharing strengthens our faith and commitment to prayer.

Many people, like this woman and myself, tend to shy away from speaking about our encounters with God, particularly the falling-in-love aspect. Yet the foundation of true prayer is a friendship based on affection, a relationship honed and developed with genuine appreciation for God. As in human relationships with an intense longing for the other, the affective piece usually begins to wane and slip into the background while the quality of enduring, faithful love moves to the foreground.

My experience of prayer has eventually become not so much a seeking for spiritual benefits as a rejoicing for the way God reveals love in my life and encourages me to grow. After my early years of emotional bonding with the Holy One, my love remains steady and strong, but my experience of the relationship is more that of Bernadette Farrell's song "Everyday God." I lost the feeling aspect of being *in love,* but I now experience more fully what it is like to have an ever developing relationship founded on a commitment that does not waver very often amid the ups and downs of life.

Perhaps you are reading this and thinking, "But I have never fallen in love with God. Something must be wrong with me. I've tried to be faithful to God through prayer, but I haven't had this kind of emotional connection." Not everyone who has a well-developed prayer life "falls in love" with God. Sometimes there is a pronounced drawing toward the Other, but not all prayerful relationships have this emotional dimension binding them together. Nor do they require this affective experience. What people do need is a conviction that relationship with God is an essential part of their existence. How this commitment comes about is a matter of individual experience and personality.

Sometimes the emotive piece can be present in our God-relationship, but we mistake it for something else. Some years ago, an older priest came each month for spiritual guidance. On more than one occasion he voiced his disappointment that he had not had "a big God moment" in his life. He emphasized how he tried to stay faithful to daily meditation, but he didn't think this spiritual practice was much of anything except a dry and empty effort, day after day, always struggling to stay awake and remain focused.

One day when this pastor came to share about his spiritual life, he again bemoaned the supposed meagerness of his prayer. Shortly after this, he related how things were going with other aspects of his life. How brightly his eyes lit up as he described a recent moment at Mass. He said that when he held the chalice up at the time of the consecration of bread and wine, his eyes looked beyond the chalice to the people in the pews. His voice wavered as he recalled the experience, "In that moment I felt the greatest love for the parishioners. I realized how dear they are to me and the beautiful bond we share."

I looked at the priest with a smile and inquired, "And you have never had an intimate spiritual encounter with God?" Immediately this pastor-of-the-dry-prayer realized the connection. He had looked diligently for an emotional experience within his personal prayer life but almost missed how God drew him into love through the people with whom he celebrated the Eucharist. While he had judged his prayer to be of little benefit, his inner vision was being sharpened so he could see how God was moving between the parishioners and himself.

Who Is This One with Whom I Relate?

If prayer is about entering into a relationship with God, then the question arises: how to name and relate to this One with whom we communicate? What names or metaphors do we use in our prayer to address a God of mystery, one who is accessible and touches our hearts in both formal prayer and in unexpected moments? Does it make any difference what words we use?

One thing that can hold us back in prayer is a false or a confining view of who God is. After my novice year, I related to God as a dearly loved presence, but this relationship contained an unperceived drawback. This shortcoming of mine

was directly reflective of my relationship with my dad —
although I was oblivious to this reality. A simple comment
when I was in my early thirties woke me up and changed my
outlook.

*What names or metaphors do we use
in our prayer to address a God of
mystery, one who is accessible and
touches our hearts in both formal
prayer and in unexpected moments?
Does it make any difference what
words we use?*

Several of us adults were planning to facilitate a senior
high school retreat. We tossed around ideas and discussed
what we might do. One team member suggested we use the
surrender prayer of Charles de Foucauld as the central theme.
In this prayer Foucauld abandons himself into God's hands
and expresses gratitude for whatever might happen to him.
He says he is ready to accept everything that comes his way
and asks only that God's will be done. Then Foucauld offers
his love to God and surrenders himself "without reserve and
with boundless confidence" into God's hands.

I was alarmed at the thought of using this prayer and immediately protested, "We can't ask these young people to pray
that prayer. I can't even pray it myself!" The team member
looked at me with wide eyes. With what seemed like feigned
surprise at my outcry, he asked in a light, joking voice a

question I will never forget: "That doesn't say much about who your God is, does it?" He made his point and it pierced through an inner wall I did not know I had, a wall that kept my relationship with God from being all it could be.

I gulped at the comment and could say little in response except, "Well, I just can't do it; that's all there is to it." I thought about his remark for weeks. Question after question arose. Why did I fear surrendering to the One who was central to my life? Why was I unable to place myself in the care of the God whom I believed truly did love me, the God with whom I met in prayer each day and felt a mutuality of relationship? What did I think would happen to me if I gave my all to this divine being?

As I searched my spirit and rummaged around in my personal history, I looked for memorable events and experiences that might be keeping me afraid of yielding to God. Finally I got it. The truth became clear. I realized I was afraid of two things: I wanted to do all I could to please God, to match up to the Holy One's expectations, and I feared what giving myself totally might cost me. I had to admit I was scared of the demands and difficult tests I thought God would ask of me.

Not only did I identify my fear of surrendering to God, I also discovered the source of that fear. I still did not trust God with my life because of an old message coming from the voice of my dad. My father was a man of integrity, with high ideals. He expected a lot from each of his children. Early on in life I knew he expected the best of me. When I did not come through and meet those hopes and ideals, I met with his displeasure and disappointment. The first time I recall this happening was when I was three or four years old. I had done some silly, inconsequential thing at dinner, like shoving my detested lettuce under the table. My father looked sternly as he reprimanded me, "So, is that the kind of girl you're turning out to be?"

His penetrating question crushed my heart. I loved my father. I sorely wanted to win his approval and receive his love. His words implied I had failed him, that he did not care about me nearly the way he would if I behaved better. While my current view of God has expanded to include more than that of seeing God as a male, fatherly image, at the time of this family incident the concept of *father* was central to my notion of the divine. Thus, I easily transposed my dad's comment onto what God's expectation would be. It seemed natural that God would ask me to shape up, to earn love and approval by how I behaved.

Thus it was that I entered my early thirties with this old impression hanging onto my relationship with God. No wonder I could not pray the prayer of surrender. Discovering the source of my flawed view did not change things instantly. I had miles to go before I could truly accept the reality of God's totally generous, unconditional love. After about ten more years and another challenging experience, I could say with the full voice of my inner conviction that God is always for me and never against me. I could finally believe what Paul wrote long ago: "For I am convinced that neither death nor life, nor angels, nor principalities, nor present things, nor future things, nor powers, nor height, nor depth, nor any creatures will be able to separate us from the love of Christ Jesus our Lord" (Rom. 8:38–39).

How did I eventually come to this freeing trust in God? When I turned forty, I chose to make a thirty-day retreat. With the help of a skilled spiritual guide, I prayed the Spiritual Exercises of St. Ignatius. These four weeks take the retreatant through a journey of meditation on the life and teachings of Jesus. During that month I repeatedly noticed the compassion and mercy Jesus extended to men and women. I saw how the messages and events of his life mirrored divine goodness. Through daily reflection on the Gospel texts, I slowly let go of the old message of having to earn God's love by matching up to some impossible divine expectation.

Praying the cycle of Jesus' life, death, and resurrection convinced me that no matter what happens in my life, God will always hold me in a welcoming embrace. I finally accepted that my human journey will have its hills and valleys because that is how life is. I no longer fear God as out to reward or punish me for my human failings, or sending me "tests" of suffering to prove my fidelity. Those four weeks of retreat freed me to enter into a relationship centered on unreserved love.

This view has not caused me to care less about living a moral and just life. On the contrary. More than ever, I desire that I be transformed through prayer — not because God will be disappointed with me, or love me less if I do not continue to grow spiritually. I now believe I have a lifelong divine companion who will never leave my side, who will cheer me on in my good times and grieve with me in harsh ones, who wants me to give of my best self, and who helps me daily by offering what I need to fulfill my desire to live a life modeled on the goodness and teachings of Jesus. More than ever, I want to be a woman of great love.

The Richness of Divine Mystery

Each of us travels our own journey with God. Sometimes that journey requires us to traverse back to the past to see how we have come to know the God we pray to now. We may discover our view of God is not expansive enough, that we have boxed God in, placing tight parameters around how we name and find the Sacred in our life.

During a group response time at a Lenten retreat, an older woman asked me, "Aren't you going to speak about the Holy Spirit?" At first I felt a bit chagrined by the question. Had I not spent an hour speaking about the qualities of the Holy Spirit by indicating ways the divine presence moves within the currents of our life? Had I not shown clearly enough that God's grace and guidance are continually providing us with wisdom for the journey? As these questions zoomed through my mind, I quickly sensed that the inquirer wanted and needed to hear *her* name for God used, the metaphor that gave her the greatest comfort and support. Because I had not directly used the name "Holy Spirit," she did not make the connection that the qualities of the Spirit were contained in the descriptions I used to refer to the divine.

Rather than boxing God in with a one-name-only approach, the consistent transitions of our life urge us to find alternative ways to name and relate with the Holy One. Many religious traditions carry hundreds, even thousands, of ways to name this mystery whom we label "God." Sufis have the ninety-nine most beautiful names of Allah. The Jewish and Christian scriptures provide a myriad of names and descriptions for the divine. Roman Catholic litanies, such as the one to the Sacred Heart of Jesus, contain numerous metaphors for Christ. Think of the various descriptions Jesus gave himself: servant, friend, teacher, door, truth, shepherd, healer, motherly hen, pathway of life, etc.

Humans have always sought meaningful ways to describe and relate to the vast, divine mystery known as God. Elizabeth A. Johnson describes it this way in her book *She Who Is:*

> No language about God will ever be fully adequate to the burning mystery which it signifies.... Great symbols of the divine always come into being not simply as a projection of the imagination, but as an awakening from the deep abyss of human existence in real encounter with divine being.

As we experience "the deep abyss" of our faith-journey, our naming of the Holy will be expanded and altered. Obviously, as Johnson notes, no name will ever fully embrace the totality of God. All names for the divine are inadequate and never fully sufficient, even "Abba" or "Daddy," the name Jesus used. All are human attempts to describe and connect with the One who dwells within us and among us. It is good for us to remember, as Jan Richardson puts it, "the naming of God is a journey not a destination."

The use of varying metaphors for the divine not only enhances our relationship with God; these names help us sense God touching the heart of what we are experiencing. When we are hurt or dealing with illness, comforting metaphors for the divine can ease our pain. When I was grieving, someone sent a card with the hands of Jesus holding a young lamb. This tender image led me to address God as "Gentle Shepherd" during my time of sadness. Although I do not often use that metaphor now, it helped immensely at the time when I sought comfort and assurance.

Metaphors such as "Loving Mother," "Compassionate One," "Sheltering Wings of Love," "Eternal Mystery," can sustain us in times of distress. When work issues are the focus of our prayer we can address God as "Just One," "Peace Bringer," "Eternal Truth," or "Heart of Forgiveness." Struggling parents might pray to God as "Holy Wisdom," "Loving Parent," "Patient One," or "Unconditional Love."

As we grow, our connection with God grows. When this happens, fresh qualities of the divine arise for us. Theologian Sandra Schneider tried to draw her readers beyond a staid way of addressing God as "Father, Son and Holy Spirit," and drolly commented, "God is more than two men and a bird." Schneider was not attempting to disparage the Trinity. Rather, she was hoping to expand the reader's view of God, to reinforce the belief that we can stretch beyond this basic concept. We can pray with many meaningful names and descriptions, while continuing to keep our Trinitarian foundation. Always we relate to a sacred mystery which will not be contained by only one name from our human voice.

The Gift of Grace

We are mistaken if we think we can grow spiritually by our own efforts. This is actually the opposite of how prayer "works." In prayer, we bring ourselves to the entryway of our relationship with the Holy One, but it is God "who is able to accomplish far more than all we can ask or imagine." Divine power at work in us gives us what we need in order for our prayer to be a catalyst for union and transformation (Eph. 3:20).

The divine vigor stirring within us is *grace,* the loving energy of God's movement. This gift enables us to grow into the person we are meant to be. The marvelous thing about grace is that it is freely contributed by God. We cannot force it to be given to us. We struggle fruitlessly if we try to grasp this gift in our clutches. What grace necessitates from us is our receptivity.

In her book on spiritual discernment, *I'd Say "Yes" God, If I Knew What You Wanted,* Nancy Reeves comments on the abundance of grace at our disposal and our inadequacy in being able to acquire it through our spiritual labors:

> As we walk our spiritual path, evidence of God's lavish love for us becomes more and more evident. This awareness often results in the realization of our unworthiness

to receive such a gift. This is true, and if God's love depended on our worthiness, no one would receive it. We are cherished for who we are, with all our shortcomings. This is grace. We are not used to free gifts, with no strings attached. It can produce anxiety to know that we can't control God's grace. Even though we are repeatedly told that divine grace and love will never be taken away from us, we would feel more comfortable if we could ensure its continuation.

Always divine grace draws us into relationship and encourages us into fuller life. Grace leads us into prayer and moves us out again, as the Acts of the Apostles clearly notes: "But you will receive power when the Holy Spirit comes upon you and you will be my witnesses in Jerusalem, throughout all Judea and Samaria, to the ends of the earth" (Acts 1:8).

Jesus experienced this himself when he was being prepared for his public ministry. Luke's Gospel tells us that Jesus was "filled with the Holy Spirit... and was led by the Spirit into the desert for forty days" (Luke 4:1). Mark's Gospel gives a stronger emphasis by saying "the Spirit *drove* him out into the desert" (Mark 1:12). Whether led or driven by the Spirit, we know that the loving movement of the Holy One was with Jesus, leading him into a place where he discovered more of his deepest self. He became increasingly sure of how God was active and alive in his being. One can imagine the intense stirring that occurred within Jesus when he lived and worked in Nazareth. He paid attention to the stirring and eventually allowed this powerful and persistent inner movement to motivate his departure from his home place and guide him into the unknown territory of the desert. In this graced wilderness, Jesus encountered the depth of his inner strength and realized where his true power lay. Jesus learned he could trust the Abba with his life.

Prayer is not a competition, not an experience of winning or of accumulating good feelings and great insights. Prayer is about "showing up" with an open mind and heart, being willing and ready to grow and change.

We, too, are led (and sometimes driven) to union with the Holy One. We cannot control, force, or manipulate our relationship with God in prayer. Like Jesus, this encounter takes place when our spirit is ripe for it. If we are ready and willing to be graced, God enters in to reach and teach us in surprising ways. Through prayer we discover how God is present to us, guiding and encouraging us along the way.

Don't Push the River

When grace entices and encourages us into an ever deepening union with God, we can be sorely tempted to want to rush and hurry the process. This hurrying and pushing is subtle and undetectable until someone points it out to us. Our overly concerted efforts in prayer often happen in the following way: we read books on prayer and spiritual growth; we listen to pastors and speakers; we observe and learn how wonderfully others are experiencing God. As all this presses in on us we leap ahead and try to put our journey with God on a fast-forward speed. We quickly forget that our prayer is numb without grace, that it remains at a standstill without the loving movement of the Spirit to give it vitality and life.

Because of pushing when "nothing seems to be happening" in our prayer, impatience, discouragement, or apathy set in. All sorts of illusionary thoughts and feelings bombard us: "Why bother?" "What's the use?" "Maybe I'm praying in the wrong way." "God has forgotten about me." "I'll never learn how to get rid of my distractions in meditation." "So and so seems much closer to God than I am." "I wish I could pray like she does." These temptations assail us when we forget that prayer is not just about our efforts but mainly about God's gracing.

Thinking that our spiritual growth is entirely up to us is not an uncommon temptation. Bridgit Mair, a psychotherapist and participant at a conference on "inner freedom" in northwest England, wrote an article in an Irish magazine. In it, she commented on her experience: "I came home from that weekend feeling nourished, replenished and connected in a way that surprised me. I had been liberated some more and it wasn't hard work, as was often customary. I hadn't been on a war footing with myself in my efforts to change or heal or transform. All I did was to turn up there, quietly open to receiving."

This comment elucidates the connection between prayer and grace. Mair's term "war footing" describes well how some people approach God and self. Prayer is not a competition, not an experience of winning or of accumulating good feelings and great insights. Prayer is about "showing up" with an open mind and heart, being willing and ready to grow and change. There is no need to get discouraged with prayer that does not match our expectations of results or prayer that reveals our sense of incompleteness.

Does prayer take effort and discipline? Yes. Every friendship requires faithful attention to the relationship. And yes, sometimes we have to *work* at renewing or restoring this bond because we have a zillion things that can lead us away from this attentiveness. But underneath, in our heart of hearts, the reason we give ourselves to the effort of prayer is love, the love that drew us in the first place into the relationship, and which is destined to unite us with God. Prayer flows from a conviction that we will do all we can to benefit this relationship and enhance its quality. In the end, however, we know that when we have done our part, God will take care of the rest. Knowing this, we attend to our prayer with surrendered peacefulness. Wise woman and author Paula D'Arcy refers to this surrender in *Sacred Threshold*:

> "Don't push the river," says my friend Richard Rohr. Don't get ahead of your soul. The goal isn't to get somewhere. The goal isn't about forcing something to

happen. The goal is to be in harmony with the gifts that are already given. The goal is to fall in love with your life.

A river flows along toward its destination easily and surely, as long as big obstacles are not placed in its path. As we enter the river of our prayer and spiritual growth, we do not need to hurry this river or shove our desire for God along like a warrior fighting in combat. Our union with God will grow in its own good time. We cannot force inner change. What we *can* do is continue to enter the relationship through prayer and keep renewing the intention of our heart to be in union with God. We can focus on the wonder of this relationship and be grateful for the beauty and graciousness of grace. And always we can keep our minds and hearts receptive and ready to receive.

Each day the river of our prayer steadily carries us along on our journey with God. Andrew Harvey offers encouragement to stay on this journey when he writes in *The Way of Passion*:

> The only way by which we unite ourselves to the Divine in us is by longing with every cell of our body and our mind to be one with the Beloved. It is the only way. And that longing has to be perpetual, permanent, it has to go on as a river in the heart, a cry in the heart, saying endlessly, "Take me to you, take me to you."

When we tend our God-relationship with love and devotion, "take me to you" becomes our theme song. This cry in our heart echoes resoundingly in the Beloved's heart as we travel the wide river of life.

Questions

1. How would you describe your relationship with God?

2. What people, circumstances, and resources have helped you most in learning how to pray?

3. What does "grace" mean to you? How have you experienced "grace" in prayer?

4. With what do you most agree, or disagree, in this chapter?

Prayer

Divine Companion,
you are ever near as I travel
on the vast river of our relationship.
Thank you for your grace in my life.
May I grow daily in my love for you.
I renew my commitment
to have you be the center of my life.
I pledge my faithfulness
to communicate with you every day.
Amen.

The Tidal Patterns of Prayer

The rolling rhythm
of the boundless sea
washes over
small, gray stones
tossed upon the sandy beach.

Wave after successive wave
draws the surrendered stones
back and forth, back and forth,
until they lift their voices
in pebbled harmony.

Then the music of the stones
settles
into momentary
silence,

rests
in the cradle of the sea's cadence,
enraptured
in the pause before the great water
turns, moves them outward,
drawing them beyond
the comforting beach,

toward the vague darkness
of the deep sea's mystery.

In such a way, the Beloved
gathers the gray pebbles of my prayer,
stirs the endless rhythm of grace,
until my heart, too, circles and
tumbles with the cadence of love.

Like gray stones on the beach
my soul dances
in the movement, rests in the silence,
then takes the emptying journey
into darkness,

there to remain in trust,
waiting to be drawn
toward the welcoming shores
of consolation.

—Joyce Rupp

I have stilled and quieted my soul
like a weaned child.
Like a weaned child on its mother's lap
so is my soul within me. (Ps. 131:2)

O NE SUNNY AFTERNOON my friend Nancy and I walked
along the beach, mostly being quiet as we enjoyed the
sea's peaceful rhythm. At one point, Nancy turned and remarked, "Did you ever notice how the ocean rests, just for a
little while, before the tide turns?" Not having spent lots of
time by the sea, that realization eluded me. From then on, I
listened more keenly. Sure enough, if one is really attentive
there is a brief, beautiful lull, a momentary stillness when the
changing of the tide occurs.

Once in awhile we get to experience in prayer this exquisite
place of "contemplative rest" when our inner tide also turns.
During this peaceful space, be it a minute, a day, a week,
a month, or longer, we receive the marvelous gift of slipping easily into awareness of God's presence. No effort is
needed. These "rests" usually do not last very long. Most of
our prayer is similar to the ocean's high and low tides, regularly slipping in and out, emptying and filling as they move
back and forth from the shore.

The flow of alternating rhythms in prayer is to be expected, yet these emptying and filling movements are rarely
welcomed. A part of us refuses to accept the ebb and flow
pattern, chiding ourselves for being unable to make our experience of God work as we want. The empty, unsettling
times of low tide appear to rob us of our experience of divine

love when, instead, these rhythms are an intrinsic part of the developing relationship.

It is natural for our prayer to have a tidal pattern. No two days of our life are exactly the same. Every day the world varies a bit, and so do we. The sun rises and sets, but no two sunrises and sunsets are identical. If nothing else, we are always a day older every time we rise in the morning. Even when our prayer appears to be one long stretch of sameness, there is still some activity, some unobtrusive shifting in our relationship with God and self.

There are numerous reasons for the emotional and mental fluctuations that take place on our inward journey. The seas of struggle and waters of turmoil in our life are bound to influence the state of our prayer. Death of a loved one, divorce, depression, job problems and financial stress, child-raising difficulties, medical issues, religious doubts, alienation with church structures, endless bad news on the political and world scene — any of these can signal shifts in the tenor of prayer.

Another significant influence for low tides in our communion with God is the inexplicable movement of *the dark night of the soul* — a time when the divine waters seem to recede completely. During this low tide, even the desire to pray may flee from our spirit. We wonder if the tide will ever turn to fill the empty shore. But this tide, too, is part of the natural movement toward greater love and wholeness. Gerald May writes that this night of the soul "is the secret way in which God not only liberates us from our attachments and idolatries, but also brings us to the realization of our true nature."

Joyful, happy periods of peace and contentment also affect the temperament of our relationship with God. These serene sojourns tend to move our internal tide toward gratitude and solace. The shores of our prayer fill with inspired consolation as the rhythm of our inner sea exudes harmony and ease.

The changing tides in prayer also include movements of ennui and lassitude, which are quite different from those lovely moments of "rest" in the utter stillness of contemplation. This kind of quiet comes from being lazy, from sloughing off desire to do anything in prayer that requires presence and concentration. We become spiritual couch potatoes. (A classic term for this in spiritual lingo is *acedia*.)

Confusing Good Feelings with Good Prayer

Confusing good feelings with good prayer is another obstacle that keeps us from accepting the natural flow of prayer's ups and downs. Some message persists in filling our mind with the false belief that if we could only "pray right," then we would always feel an easy, overwhelming peace. The goal of prayer is not to *pray right,* nor is it to have constant noble and inspiring thoughts, nor to have a pleasant sameness where we never have any distractions. The goal is to have *healthy* prayer, prayer that transforms us.

German theologian Dorothee Soelle maintains that prayer is about our becoming egoless. In other words, the focus of our prayer is less and less on us and more and more on who God is and how, in Soelle's words, "we live out God" in our day-to-day life. She quotes Martin Buber as saying, "Success is not a name of God." Soelle follows up with the comment:

"To let go of the ego means, among other things, to let go of the coercion to succeed."

The ego always wants to succeed, to believe it can take control so things go well. It wants to be in charge, to determine what thoughts and feelings are activated when we pray. Our ego tries to convince us that success is the criterion by which to judge our prayer as effective. The ego aims for the "success" of stopping the ebb and flow pattern, seeks the flowing in, the filling up, the effervescence of consolation and positive emotional response.

If we listen closely, we might hear the ego whimper when the tide goes out in our prayer. When emotions such as emptiness, confusion, restlessness, irritability, disappointment, and sadness are present, the ego becomes alarmed. When this happens, the ego often urges self-recrimination, fault-finding, questioning, and blaming. We then try to figure out what "went wrong" with the way we prayed and how we can pray in such a way that we regain the mental and emotional responses we consider worthy. This type of frustration came through in a letter I received via my website:

> When I pray, I "believe" God is listening, but there have only been two or three times in my life when I actually "felt" His very presence there with me. I am ALWAYS struggling to find a way to get back to that place. Those times coincided with times when I was most needy/empty. Perhaps that had something to do with it. I feel, though, that I *should* be able to get back to Him — into His presence — but I never really do. It's very frustrating. I go through all the motions, read all

the right stuff, even go to workshops and retreats; I try every "type" of prayer I read about, etc. I'm not saying that none of my prayer experiences have been fulfilling; some are very much so. However, I've tasted more and I want it all the time. I am in a relatively "happy" time in my life; my life is going well. It seems harder than ever to get "close" to God.

When I responded to this letter, I encouraged her to let go of trying to make her relationship with God work the way she wanted, to trust that God knew the desire of her heart. Not having the emotional or intellectual caveats we yearn for can seem like failure or weakness to us. The ego yells, "Something's wrong!" Prayer is meant to sustain our faith, encourage our fidelity to the Beloved, and hold us steadily in that relationship, but good feelings are not always present to do that for us. Faith holds us close to God. Love keeps that link secure. We stay steadfast in prayer, no matter how the inner tide is turning. St. Paul emphasizes this in his letter to the Romans: "The Spirit too comes to the aid of our weakness; for we do not know how to pray as we ought, but the Spirit itself intercedes with inexpressible groanings. And the one who searches the heart, knows what is the intention of the Spirit" (Rom. 8:26–27).

A true reverence for the other and a respect based on love strong enough to accept the other in his or her totality is basic to the faithfulness and growth of friendship. Likewise, learning to trust God with our life, with the essence of who and how we are, is imperative. As we reach forth to the divine, the divine reaches forth to us. Mutual love ignites and sustains this relationship.

Surrendering to the Great Mystery

All spiritual growth is fraught with mystery. No matter how hard we try, we cannot push and shove our way into union with the Holy One. We can only give ourselves fully to the loving movement of God. The same woman who wrote to me about her frustration in not having good feelings in prayer, no matter what she tried to do, sent me another letter some weeks later. Her experience describes what can occur when we allow God's grace to take over. She wrote after returning from a four-day silent retreat in which she listened to God's desires for her instead of demanding that her desires be met:

> I had quite a cathartic experience there. Your insight was among a few others I discovered while allowing myself the opportunity to truly be alone with God and listen. I actually found exactly what I had been longing for in a very unexpected but real — like a "two-by-four upside the head" real way.

What a challenge we face in being unable to force God's way in our spiritual growth. Jesus addressed this issue when he spoke about the kingdom of God being as steady and silent as a seed awaiting its birth into new life: "It is as if a [farmer] were to scatter seed on the land and would sleep and rise night and day and the seed would sprout and grow, [one] knows not how. Of its own accord the land yields fruit, first the blade, then the ear, then the full grain in the ear" (Mark 4:27–28).

We cannot compel our love to germinate and mature any more than the farmer can force the seed to green and grow. A seed has its own time. After it is planted the farmer trusts the seed lying in the darkness to eventually give way to a new shoot of life. How true this is of prayer when we plant the seed of love and hope that it will grow. The seed in the dark soil looks much the same from day to day until the husk breaks open and a tiny green bit of life starts to show itself. To look at the seed in the seemingly empty days before it breaks open, one would think absolutely nothing is happening. When we open our heart in love to God we are like the seed, waiting for our spiritual germination.

A resource that inspires me toward greater confidence in God is a book containing the diaries of Etty Hillesum, a young Jewish woman who died at Auschwitz in November 1943 at the age of twenty-nine. *An Interrupted Life* candidly reveals Etty's developing relationship with God. As she is caught in the fray of the Holocaust, Etty inches closer and closer to the One whom she searched and desired to know in her earlier, unsettling years of personal growth. Gradually, she surrenders her heart to God, growing certain that whatever happens, God is with her. She has faith that "somewhere there is something inside me that will never desert me again." A turning point comes when Etty falls on her knees to pray:

A desire to kneel down sometimes pulses through my body, or rather it is as if my body had been meant and made for the act of kneeling. Sometimes, in moments of deep gratitude, kneeling down becomes an overwhelming urge, head deeply bowed, hands before my face.

Whether we physically kneel is not nearly as important as our kneeling inwardly. What matters is whether we acknowledge our dependency upon God to grow and change us, to lead us into a love that knows no conditions or bounds. Jesus came to his own peace with this through his process of surrendering. In the Garden of Olives Jesus yields to his Abba. Again, when he hangs on the cross, after first questioning if he has been abandoned in his hour of death, Jesus turns inwardly and submits his entire being, saying, "Into your hands I commend my spirit" (Luke 23:46).

To look at the seed in the seemingly empty days before it breaks open, one would think absolutely nothing is happening. When we open our heart in love to God we are like the seed, waiting for our spiritual germination.

James Finley, a former student of Thomas Merton, remembers one of the famed monk's teachings regarding surrender in prayer. In *Merton's Palace of Nowhere,* Finley recalls how Merton compared *letting go* to that of a green apple on a tree. The apple does not get red, ripe, and juicy by squirming, pushing, and worrying, or by insisting that the sun shine upon it. No, the apple waits attentively while it remains open to receive the juice from the root sending nutrients up through the tree, waits while the warmth of the sun's radiance transforms it. Eventually, the green apple grows into a delicious fruit ready for harvest.

Opening to God

Whenever I lead retreats one of the first things I ask participants to do is "pray to be open." If there is openness, wondrous transformation can take place. If the mind or heart is closed, little can happen. If our spirit remains blocked, we end up holding on to our weaknesses and self-absorptions, misjudging the goodness of God, refusing to trust, and insisting on having our own way. Divine love waits for us to let go of our hesitancies and resistances so we can freely receive what is being offered.

Growth through prayer requires us to release thoughts, feelings, and behaviors that hold us back from discovering our true self. To be open in prayer is to be willing to acknowledge the totality of who we are, to divest of what no longer adequately serves our life and our God-relationship. In his book *With Open Hands,* Henri Nouwen describes this movement by telling the story of a woman in a psychiatric center who would not let go of a coin clutched in her clammy, tight fist. Nouwen comments:

> When you are invited to pray, you are asked to open up your tightly clenched fist and give up your last coin. But who wants to do that? A first prayer, therefore, is often a painful prayer because you discover you don't want

to let go. You hold fast to what is familiar, even if you aren't proud of it.... When you want to pray, then, the first question is: How do I open my clenched hands? Certainly not by violence. Nor by a forced decision. Perhaps you can find your way to prayer by carefully listening to the words the angel spoke to Zechariah, Mary, the shepherds, and women at the tomb: "Don't be afraid."

Fear can keep us clinging to our old ways. Fear also keeps us from embracing new ways. How well I remember the fear I felt when I moved toward a new way of meditation. For over thirty years my morning prayer focused on pondering the daily scripture passages. Then there came a time when the words of scripture (actually any words at all) crowded the silence that drew me into the stillness of God. Meditation on scripture always seemed the best way. Now there I was, sensing the need to let go of this mode of prayer and move into a non-verbal, non-thinking, more contemplative way to be with my divine companion. I was scared I would lose the insights scripture provided. I was frightened to detach from the security of thoughts.

When we acknowledge fear's presence, it does not immediately disappear. For several years, I struggled in and out of meditation and contemplation. Eventually, trust in God became stronger than my hesitations. I was able to let go and enter where I was being led — away from the comfort of inspiring ideas and into the open space of simply *being with* God. In the process, I discovered that scripture could still reach and teach me but at times other than during contemplative prayer.

When I was struggling with the move to a more contemplative approach, I was fortunate to have a wise spiritual guide accompanying me. Spiritual guides are helpful for many reasons, particularly because of the tendency to judge the experience of prayer falsely. We have our own preconceived notions about how we ought to pray and about whether our growth is, or is not, happening. Thus, we cannot stand outside our self to see the truth clearly. An objective person listens and encourages us to remain faithful in the midst of prayer's diverse rhythms.

My spiritual director spoke with me about "letting go" and encouraged me to detach from my old way of praying. Detachment is often misunderstood as meaning one has to let go completely or to stop caring and become separate from what one enjoys. Quite the opposite is true. Angeles Arrien describes detachment in *The Four-Fold Way* as "the capacity to care deeply from an objective place." She explores this notion further and remarks that true detachment urges us to invest fully but that we also need to *"be open to outcome, not attached to outcome."*

In prayer we come with a heart centered on the One we love. We give ourselves as fully as possible to this Great Love but we do not clutch on to the results of that loving relationship. In my situation, I was still fully invested in my relationship with God, but I had to let go of what I expected from it when I moved into another mode of prayer. I had to put my faith in the process, stay open, and leave the outcome to God.

Staying Faithful to Daily Prayer

People are troubled when they cannot hold on to the consolations they desire in their efforts to pray. They want to constantly sense God's nearness so that personal prayer is cushy and undemanding. Instead of this, God moves through our prayer at a pace other than what we want or expect. When we do not accept this pace, there is struggle year after year. When life gets full, the first thing to fly off the daily schedule is usually the time set aside for prayer. (Foregoing prayer is much easier to do when seemingly little fruit appears to be coming from it.)

Faithfulness is about finding a place of peace within us that trusts in God's nearness, no matter whether we *feel* this nearness or not. We go on praying whether the tide is in or out. We "let go and let God," who knows the intention of our heart. And that is enough.

When we pray, we cross a threshold into mystery. We enter openly, with an assurance that our life will continually take on the hue of the Holy One. In order to do this, we need quiet times, spaces in our day or evening when silence and solitude are given prominence in our schedule. Our culture does not promote this silence. On the contrary. We are constantly pulled this way and that by our overly active society. The electronic age seduces us with constant noise and frenetic, compulsive action. Only with steadfast determination will we create the space we need for daily, formal prayer.

At an early December retreat in northern California, I asked those present to name their greatest impediment to spiritual growth. Many of them spoke about "busyness" and "lack of time" as the central obstacles. Not surprising. This challenge has to be addressed if one is to be faithful to daily prayer. I've noticed how increasingly uncomfortable adults at retreats are with even a half hour of silence. Although I provide a whole page of scripture passages, a list of suggested questions and activities for the reflection time, they soon become restless and start carrying on conversations or talking on their cell phones.

When we slow down and allow for quiet spaces, there are fewer barriers between us and the Holy One. In stillness, we come face to face with what we might otherwise miss or avoid. As we give ourselves to periods of silence and solitude, we uncover more of the truth that guides our life and are able to relish the goodness of the Beloved dwelling within the beauty of our soul.

Dawna Markova, a respected developer of learning centers, discovered the value of alone time with God when she chose to go on a six-month solitude-retreat high in the mountains of Utah. This retreat was no easy thing. Yet she determinedly stayed with the loneliness and came forth with vision and wisdom to guide her life. During those months, Markova gained a tremendous inner strength that helped her ascertain and integrate her purpose in life. She writes:

> ... when we avoid knowing ourselves, we end up living numb, passionless lives, disconnected from our soul's true purpose. But when you have the courage to shape your life from the essence of who you are, you ignite, becoming truly alive. This requires letting go of

everything that is inauthentic. But how can you even know your truth unless you slow down, in your own quiet company?

Most of us do not have the luxury of a six-month sabbatical like Markova's. Even if we did, we might not accept doing this because of the challenge. That much silence and solitude sounds great from a distance, but once we enter into it, the experience may shake us with fear, relentless anxiety, or boredom. All of us have twenty-four hours in a day, though. Twenty-four glorious hours in which we can glean some space to set aside for quiet, where we can aim for quality time with God. We simply cannot run through our life and expect to find lasting peace and meaning. If we continue *doing and doing* we will miss those graced opportunities to grow deeper, wiser, and more loving.

When Jesus spoke about prayer, he encouraged his listeners to: " . . . go to your inner room, close the door, and pray to your Father in secret" (Matt. 6:6). Jesus practiced what he preached. The Gospels assure us that Jesus left the active, intense pace he kept and went to the mountains to commune with the One who restored his spiritual vitality. Those spaces of communion are imperative for all of us.

Distractions

Because our lives are filled with an overly abundant amount of activity, distractions often bombard us when we do finally go into our *inner room* to pray. This morning in meditation I had a distraction about "distractions." Yes, in the midst of prayer, thoughts came about what I would write here regarding the constant comings and goings of the mind when we are at prayer. When I became aware of my thoughts about *distractions*, I smiled ironically. Then I simply spoke to the distractions and said, "Thank you. Not now." I do that often when insights come that I'd like to keep. I learned my lesson one day when some marvelous thoughts came that I was certain would be "perfect" for an article that needed a good introduction. I decided to get up from my prayer cushion and write down the ideas lest they be gone forever, certain that the Spirit was giving them to me. Well, the moment I sat down in my chair, paper and pen in hand, my mind was a blank. I could not recall one single word or sentence that had deliciously floated in my head just a minute before!

The empty, unsettling times of low tide appear to rob us of our experience of divine love when, instead, these rhythms are an intrinsic part of the developing relationship.

One could fill a book about the many approaches to be taken regarding distractions in prayer. What do we do with the zillions of things that fill our heads and the countless feelings that tug at our hearts when we choose to meditate? Spiritual teachers give a myriad of suggestions. Some refer to distractions as "monkey mind" because of how active and jumpy the mind is, leaping from tree limb to tree limb of thought. They insist we quiet this activity by emptying the mind of everything. Other teachers promote focusing the mind by using a word, or a phrase, to stay centered on union with God. Still others say, "Whatever thoughts and feelings are there, don't judge them as good or bad, just notice them. Let them come and go." Marc Ian Barasch tells of a spiritual teacher who suggested treating distractions like a doorman at a hotel. The doorman lets people in but does not follow them down the hall, and when the doorman lets people out the door he does not follow them down the street.

The mind is a marvelous gift and we do not want to disparage it in any way when attempting to pray. What we do need is to keep our mind from taking over in our prayer. There is no one, easy, "foolproof" solution to take care of distractions. Most of the time we need to ignore what circles around in our head and heart, but sometimes we need to listen to it. If we have a steady stream of upset feelings or hostile thoughts, this may be a call to reconciliation, nonjudgment, or letting go. If our distractions offer insights into how we can be of service to others, maybe God is leading us to generosity and a fuller giving of ourselves.

The Breath of God

I have never been able to empty my mind of all that stirs within it. Perhaps I never will be able to do so. Maybe it is not necessary. Maybe it is impossible. What I *can* do in prayer is to place my focus elsewhere, to channel my mental and emotional energies in another direction, doing what I can to continually return to the intention of being in union with God. Paying attention to my breathing is one way to do this.

The pattern of the breath helps me stay focused when distractions circle the wagons of my mind. This ancient practice stems from a variety of spiritual traditions that teach about using the pattern of breath when we are meditating.

Like the tidal pattern of the sea, breathing is a steady rhythm of "in and out" leading to peaceful concentration. Hildegard of Bingen, a sixteenth-century mystic, described prayer as "joining the in-breath with the out-breath to the One Breath of the universe." Henri Nouwen suggested: "There is probably no image that expresses so well the intimacy with God in prayer as the image of God's breath."

In *The Illuminated Prayer*, the renowned Sufi teacher Bawa's description of prayer also speaks of this finely focused practice of being attentive: "Yearning for God in every thought, directing every breath toward the One, intending no harm, that is prayer." When my beloved spiritual director lay dying, three weeks after being diagnosed with lung cancer, I thought of Bawa's *directing every breath toward the One*. Sitting by Jennifer's bedside, I listened to her labored breathing and watched the slow, rhythmic rise and fall of her chest. The steady in and out pattern of Jennifer's inhalations and exhalations filled the room with a discernible tranquility. Despite my sadness, a gentle comfort filled me. I knew we were united by the history of our spiritual journeying and, also, by a profound communion through the very air we breathed and shared.

Breath is absolutely essential for life. It is an innate part of us. We breathe without thinking about the process unless we have asthma or other lung and heart difficulties. Basil of Caesarea, a fourth-century bishop, envisioned the Spirit as *the Breath of God* in his great work, *On the Holy Spirit.* Basil compared the Spirit's movement within us to our natural breath coming into us from the earth's atmosphere and leaving our lungs to reenter the larger sphere of life. For Basil, God is as near to us as every breath we take. Author Denis Edwards develops Basil's understanding of the Spirit as the one who brings creatures into communion with the divine in his book *Breath of Life:*

> ... the Spirit is the presence of God to creation, the immanence of God. The immanent Breath of God is always in communion with the Word and the Source of All. But it is the Spirit's role to dwell in creatures, creating the bond of communion between the creature and the life of God. The Spirit is the Communion-Bringer and, as such, is the Life-Giver and Sanctifier.

Thus, our breath constantly provides a reminder of our communion with God. The pattern of our breathing presents an attentive focus in prayer, keeping us mindful of the One who dwells with us. The in-and-out of breathing assures us that whatever our mental and emotional state in prayer, we are always held within the great rhythm of Eternal Love. Awareness of our breath also serves to remind us that every inhalation and exhalation of ours joins us to the Great Breath in one vast outpouring of love in the universe.

Yielding to the Changing Tides

As I look at my own history of experiencing prayer, I find a constant movement of high and low tides, numerous ups and downs, mountains and valleys, emptying and filling, and always some brief resting phases. There have been periods when all I could do was allow struggle and sorrow onto my barren shore, lean on God in faith, and try to be true to my daily spiritual practice. In the midst of those long periods of spiritual drought, fleeting joy surprised me in the beauty of nature and the kindness of people. Likewise, in the fluctuating tides of prayer when I experienced delicious contentment and almost effortless communion with God, certain turns within the day or week affected my peaceful prayer. These events catapulted my mind into endless distraction and shoved my emotions into fraught feelings of distress and disquiet.

As I grow older, these variations of disposition and inner atmosphere continue in my prayer life. What has changed is my attitude and approach to this rhythm. I am slowly learning the necessity of entering into the pattern with my whole heart and trusting God to be there with me. I am gradually yielding to the tides of prayer. When the changes come, I let them come. I pay attention to what is happening. If annoyance or heartache arise and I need to deal with personal issues, I do. If joy and contentment persist, I gratefully accept these movements without trying to cling. When those little hushes and rests arrive for a brief stay, everything in me wants to shout "hurrah," but the moment I revel in them, the lovely stillness is gone, so I simply welcome them for however long they remain.

I am firmly convinced that whatever the movement in prayer, God is with me. My prayer has value even if I may never know exactly how the effect of this prayer will show its face. Like a surfer on the great waters of life, the waves of grace constantly return to bring me to the waiting shores of peace.

Questions

1. How have you experienced the "tidal patterns" (the fluctuating fullness and emptiness) in prayer?

2. What are your greatest challenges and obstacles in prayer?

3. What are your thoughts and feelings in regard to surrendering to the mystery of God?

4. With what do you most agree, or disagree, in this chapter?

Prayer

Breath of Life,
You ride the waves of life with me
in the rhythms of my communion with you.
You enter the comings and goings
of each day and in every prayer I breathe.
Whether I am in the stillness of quiet prayer
or in the fullness of the day's activity,
may your peace flow through my being.
Amen.

Keeping the Vigil of Mystery

Begin again, and again,
and again,
deliberately, with intention,
each day

opening the heart's door,
seeking to unite
with the divine companion,
eager to abide with us.

Stop squirming.
Release clinging.
Let go of the binding chains
to self-willed ways.

Begin again, and again,
and again,
with ardent faith
and endless vigil.

Never give up on praying.

Countless are the paths
leading to the heart's home

where Ancient Love
anticipates us,

waiting, always waiting,
while our restless heart turns
inward, as we listen

for the whisper
of remembrance,
the taste of an Eternal One
here, yet, far,

the fragrance of the divine breath,
for a few delicious
moments, touching our soul.

— Joyce Rupp

To live with the Spirit of God is to be a listener.
It is to keep the vigil of mystery,
earthless and still.
One leans to catch the stirring of the Spirit,
strange as the wind's will.

— Jessica Powers

PRAYER KEEPS OUR LIFE breathing with love. In our fast-paced world, it is easy to become complacent or absentminded about the value of our inner terrain and the One who holds us in love. Even when we remain focused and faithful to this relationship, we can slip into routines and habits that blunt the energy we bring to prayer. Like furniture in a house, our approach and practice of prayer occasionally needs a good dusting off. How much brighter the details of an object when the accumulation of dust is brushed away. So, too, with prayer.

When we review our prayer, we notice if it has lost its shine or possibly deteriorated. By holding our daily spiritual practice up to the light of honesty, we observe if we are putting our whole heart and soul into it. We look to see if there are ways we might more fully connect with God. We also relearn how beneficial it is to be a listener to the deep mystery of the Holy One and notice how we are maturing into love through the Spirit's presence in us.

One evening when theologian and creative storyteller John Shea was speaking, he queried:

I wonder if our prayers and our liturgies are really times of changed consciousness...if they are times where we do not strain any longer, where our rituals, our liturgies, our prayer forms, really allow us to go deep within ourselves and rest for a moment, in order to once again take up the struggle of life, or have our liturgies and our prayer forms become just another way where awareness is strained, pulled out of ourselves, alienated?...Is it really a time when we come home to the deepest center of ourselves where the human spirit opens into the divine spirit?

In this chapter, I invite you to join me in "doing some dusting" by recalling some of the underpinnings and components to prayer. My goal in doing this is to enable our prayer to become what Shea suggests, a time of coming home to our deepest center where, in Jessica Powers's poetic words, we "keep the vigil of mystery."

Intention

Having a conscious *intention* to be at prayer is vital if we are to come home to that inner place of unity and peace to which God invites us. *Intention* means that right here, right now, before beginning to pray, we deliberately set as our purpose that of being in relationship with God. *Intention* implies a conscious choice of remembering this beloved presence. We intentionally move our awareness toward our deepest center, even if our wandering mind and listless heart challenge our desire to do so.

As with much of my growth in prayer, I learned the value of *setting an intention* only after I had a humbling experience. This recognition happened after a whole week went by in which I was faithful every day to a half hour of meditation. At the end of the week, to my chagrin, I realized that never once had I been deliberate about entering into a relationship with God. Oh, I had "prayed" each day. I had gone through the motions, the routine. I was *physically* present, but my mind and heart were never *purposefully* connected with the Holy One. My prayer was like living with someone all week but never making an effort to become aware of the other person's presence.

Since that time, the first thing I do when beginning my prayer time is to intentionally acknowledge the indwelling of the Holy One. This recognition does not take long, no more than greeting an old and dear friend. A simple remembrance is all that is needed: "Hello, I know I am not alone. I believe you are with me. I intend to be united with you now. I desire to give myself to you with love."

Temples of God

We are never alone in prayer. Wherever and whenever we pray, we enter this experience as temples of the sacred. It is easy to overlook this comforting reality. The question St. Paul asked the Corinthians is one that continually sits on the doorstep of our prayer: "Do you not know that you are the temple of God, and that the Spirit of God dwells in you?" (1 Cor. 3:16). We abide in the Holy One and the Holy One

abides in us (John 15:4). Deliberate recognition of this presence assures us that even if we *feel* separated, the Spirit is
there with us.

A lovely print by an unknown artist sits by my daily place
of meditation. I keep this image nearby to remind me that
the Beloved has a home in the deepest core of my being. In
the print, a woman with a smooth, almond-shaped face and
flowing black hair frames her small hands around the sides of
her heart from which bright rays of light radiate, reminiscent
of the divine light. The background around the woman's head
is permeated with a glow of soft light.

Daphne Rose Kingma describes *soul* as "the divine frag-
ment within us . . . the energy, the beauty and eternity of pure
love. It is our essence." Scripture assures us that our soul is
filled with the Spirit's loving energy and radiant goodness. The
soul is a great ally within our "earthenware jars" where the
"surpassing power of God" fills us with tremendous resiliency
(2 Cor. 4:7).

Gerald May notes that the two great teachers of prayer,
St. John of the Cross and St. Teresa of Avila, believed firmly
that union with God is not something that we work at to
make happen. They teach that this union already exists due
to the indwelling of the Spirit within us. The greatest difficulty
in prayer, as Teresa names it, is that people do not believe God
is with them. I wonder, given our current hectic culture, if it
is not so much *doubt* about God's being with us as it is an
unawareness of this profound presence that prevents prayer
from happening. We can believe all sorts of things about the
necessity of prayer but lock the door on those convictions

through our whirlwind of endless busyness. We may want to grow deeper and stronger in our God-relationship but get caught in a plethora of activities and expectations, quickly losing awareness of the tremendous gift residing in us. "I'm afraid that too often we leave the deeps of life untouched," writes Percy Ainsworth, "not because we remember they are sacred but because we forget they are there."

Awareness

Awareness has long been a challenge for those desiring to pray. Being alert to who God is and to what stirs within us requires undivided attentiveness. The poet Kabir compares spiritual inattentiveness to a fish in the water that is thirsty. Rumi, another Sufi writer, parallels lack of awareness to that of going hungry even though there is a basket of bread on one's head. Jesus also encourages awareness by urging his followers to "look" and "listen."

The Gospels tell us a great deal about the attentiveness of Jesus. He is both internally and externally aware. His parables and lessons contain details from everyday life, details he could only have gleaned by carefully observing birds, camels, fig trees, mustard seeds, flowers, needles, pearls, and other things around him. Likewise, Jesus is alert to the inner resonance of those who come to him. Scripture recounts how Jesus listened keenly and "realized the intentions of their hearts" (Luke 5:22; 6:8; 9:47). This inner awareness of Jesus is evident in countless encounters, including his perception of goodness in the Samaritan woman, his recognition of the jealousy and antipathy in his enemies' hearts, and his sensing someone had come up from behind him and touched the hem of his robe.

In order to be aware and listen closely to God, we need an alert attentiveness. Constant running and hurrying does not contribute to our spiritual well-being when it keeps us from paying attention to the deeper meaning inherent in life. Not all see it this way. In an article titled, "Finding God in the Busyness," Canadian writer Maura Hanrahan challenges the need for retreats, as well as for definite times of personal reflection and prayer. She maintains that it is enough to be with God amid the busyness:

> But there is also the implication that quiet and withdrawal are pre-requisites for spiritual health. So many people have bought the notion that it is only in silence and solitude that we can connect to the spiritual, to God. Consequently, there are people who sincerely believe that they have to disconnect from their real lives to connect with God. But this is not so.

There is partial truth to Hanrahan's assertion that not everyone needs to go away to pray. Extended times of prayer, such as retreats, can be a marvelous help for developing our relationship with God, but this is not what is most vital for spiritual growth. Many people cannot leave home, family, or work for the luxury of a retreat, but everyone can find a bit of space in the day for a mini-retreat, a small portion of twenty-four hours allotted for personal prayer. Hanrahan too easily dismisses this essential element when she focuses on how God is found within the whirlwind of life. Without some quiet reflection, some solitude and stillness, our inner eyes will eventually be too blurred and weary to discover God in the rushing of our demanding days.

Hanrahan makes a good point about not having to disconnect from "our real lives" in order to pray. Relationship with God is not about one or the other — either retreating from busyness or finding God within the busyness. Both personal prayer *and* the fullness of life nourish our love for God and God's love for us. The rest of our life is not a block to this affectionate relationship. Rather, all of life is a doorway to the divine, but we need reflective awareness for these doors to open.

Listening to the Spirit's Stirrings

The psalmist prays, "My heart is steadfast, O God, my heart is steadfast. Awake, my soul!...I will awake the dawn" (Ps. 57:7–9). How do we awaken our soul? How do we walk through the door of our full lives and permit God to rouse the innermost part of ourselves? One of the central ways to do this is to wean ourselves from our non-attention and develop our ability to become keen listeners.

One summer day I sat on the back porch fully immersed in preparing a talk for a conference on "listening to God." As I leaned over my notebook, I heard a bird singing a penetrating, melodious song. The warbling went on and on, but I did not bother to look or listen because I was concentrating on my work. Finally, an inner stirring drew me to put my pen down.

I thought, "Listen! Stop what you are doing! Pay attention to this beautiful song. It is too glorious to miss." I looked up to find the source of the singing and saw a female house-finch seated at the bird feeder and a male finch perched on a branch nearby. The male finch was singing to the female who was busily grooming her little feet and preening her feathers. She pretended to peck at the food in the feeder, seemingly ignoring the enticing song. Finally, the female finch lifted up and flew away. The moment she left the feeder, the other bird's beautiful music stopped.

Without some quiet reflection, some solitude and stillness, our inner eyes will eventually be too blurred and weary to discover God in the rushing of our demanding days.

As I watched the scene, I thought, "God is always singing a love song, desiring to get my attention, wanting to let me know I am cherished, but I get absorbed in my activity. Like the female bird, I peck and clean, all the while ignoring or missing the beauty of the divine song and the One who sings it." Only by listening to the melody of God will I recognize and respond to what is beneath the external aspects of my life. Only then will I turn my heart more fully toward the One who calls insistently to me.

Meister Eckhart, enigmatic and influential German mystic, wisely noted, "God is at home. We are the ones who have gone out for a walk." How true this is. God is continually trying to communicate with us if only we will take notice. Mary, mother of Jesus, listened closely to what the Beloved was singing to her. No foot pecking or feather preening for Mary. On several occasions the Gospels tell us that Mary "kept all these things, reflecting on them in her heart" (Luke 2:19, 51). Mary was acutely attuned to the Holy One's movement within her. Prayer requires the same from us.

When we listen as Mary did, we may not always like what we hear. The stirrings that come in our attentive listening sometimes turn us in a direction we least expect, as it did for Mary. Being alert and watchful does not guarantee that the content of our prayer will lack struggle and uncertainty. Even the finest of quality praying does not give instant solutions to problems or clear responses to questions.

When we choose to pray, we choose to grow. This growth is not always harmonious and comfortable. Yet if we stay awake and remain faithful to praying each day, peace and harmony will eventually be the result of our prayer as it was in Mary's encounter with the Spirit. In spite of this reality, who of us is not tempted occasionally to let our personal prayer slip by the wayside either because we do not want the discomfort it affords us, or because we let our overly full schedules push it out of the way?

We are kidding ourselves if we think we can consistently dismiss daily prayer and still maintain a quality relationship with the Holy One. Prayer opens the space of our inner being so we can be more fully attentive to divine nudgings throughout the day. There was a time when my ministerial life was so heaped up with things to do that I thought I could not possibly afford time in the day for personal prayer. My spiritual director helped change my attitude. She suggested making an appointment with myself each day and be firm about keeping it. She also wisely recommended setting aside an evening a week, and a day a month, for more extended reflection and prayer. I was to write my name in my appointment book on the times and days I chose. This was some of the best advice I ever received. Without her sound counsel, I would have lived on the surface of life, been burned out in my work, and experienced my relationship with God thinning to a weak patch of disconnectedness.

Developing an ability to listen to the Spirit's movements requires practice. We may never find it easy to do. Some people are fearful of silence and seek to fill the space with music, television, conversation, words, anything but utter stillness. Others think they cannot pray unless they do away with the smallest sound around them. When choosing a time and place of prayer, it is helpful to have a quiet area, but this may not always be possible in our noisy world. So, instead, we learn to become silent inside our self and pray amid external noise we can neither quell nor control.

Recently, I was meditating with a group of young adults. The small chapel we were in was not far from a clattering kitchen where parishioners were preparing a church dinner. I encouraged us to not treat the sound coming from the kitchen as our enemy but rather to simply be aware of the sound. Trying to get rid of the noise would only lead to frustration and a waste of good energy. I reminded the young adults that there was no need to fuss about being unable to have "perfectly quiet space." We were praying in the midst of life. At the end of our meditation, the group readily acknowledged that the kitchen racket gradually became a background rather than a foreground to our prayer, and no longer interfered with concentration.

Anthony DeMello, S.J., once remarked, "The present moment is never unbearable if you live in it fully. What is unbearable is to have your body here at 10:00 a.m. and your mind at 6:00 p.m., your body in Bombay and your mind in San Francisco." Our acceptance of the world in which we pray allows us to peacefully be present, to not judge obtrusive sounds like cars honking, dogs barking, loud music blaring, or children raucously at play as anything other than the sounds of life. Complete silence and solitude, a rested body, an undistracted mind are bonuses for prayer, but we cannot wait until these conditions are fully present before we decide to pray. Who knows but what God may communicate with us in the very things we want to eliminate?

Cluttered Prayer

Although we may not be able to get rid of unwanted clamor in the arena of our prayer, we can remove some hindrances, like trying to bring too much into it. A woman who has since become a dear friend of mine came to me years ago asking for help in learning how to use scripture for prayer. Her faithfulness to daily prayer was already remarkable. She never failed to rise early and pray in the solitude of predawn. During her years of doing this, she accumulated all sorts of little prayers created by others that she said each morning. In the course of her prayer time she went from one booklet to another with no gaps in between to breathe and listen to the voice of the Holy One. Word after word tumbled out of her, creating a landfill of chatter that interfered with her ability to hear the Spirit because she was too busy reading the extensive amount of written words. This cluttered prayer time kept her from moving deeper into her soul-space and listening to the mystery within it.

There is nothing wrong with written prayers and little prayer books. These can be helpful tools for communicating with God, but when they become one long string of continuous intercession and endless verbiage, with no space for silence, they prevent us from listening and receiving what the Spirit wants to communicate. When Jesus spoke about prayer he warned those he taught to not babble on and on (Matt. 6:7). This deeply prayerful woman gradually moved away from her stack of prayers to using just a few of them. In doing so, she now has time to find peace and guidance by attentively listening to the Holy One.

Cluttered prayer is topsy-turvy prayer in which one tumbles and fumbles. If prayer consists of numerous bits of this and that, then this lack of direction will be carried into the rest of the day in a similar vein — there will not be a strong link, a meaningful thread of thought and spiritual intention. No one has to give up booklets and rote prayers, but underneath those pieces each one needs an uncluttered inner space in order to find a focus and purpose for each day's journey.

Unexpected Prayer

Occasionally, the mystery of God enters our lives with such surprise and clarity we have no choice but to move immediately and totally toward an abiding awareness of this great love. For a brief time, we are swept up in a contemplative movement that instantly connects our inner and outer world. We cross the threshold where we meet and merge with divine presence. It is a sweet, holy, amazing moment.

A Wisconsin resident wrote and told me how he awoke one evening and went into the kitchen to get a drink of water. As he passed the refrigerator, he felt as if his body was being lifted off the floor. As this happened, John experienced the most profound peace and complete joy. A sense of God's nearness took over his entire being. He was astonished at what he felt and went over to the window where he stood with silent amazement, gazing into the dark night. John couldn't stop smiling. He eventually went back to bed, still smiling, and continued to ponder the surprising incident. Then he got up again, sat at the kitchen table and wrote about the unusual event, knowing he would otherwise disbelieve the experience was real when he got up the next morning.

I was grateful to John for sharing the special moment with me. One often hesitates telling others about this kind of thing for fear of being thought foolish or irrational. John's call to closeness with God confirmed my own sacred moment a few years earlier. On a crisp early March morning I went for my daily walk. A few blocks later, I started up a hilly street. When I looked up, I gasped a huge "Oh!" There before me was the full moon, filling up the entire end of the street and sky before me. The round, shining moon looked like it was sitting on the ground. What I remember most is an instant sense of the "biggest love" I ever knew and a feeling that I could die immediately and be completely happy.

This incident was brief, but it drew me into closer communion with the Holy One throughout that day and on into the future. Even now, as I recall the event, the strong sense of "great love" returns. None of us can plan or force these unusual situations to occur. They are *mystical moments* filled with an unexplainable intimacy, drawing us into a communion with divinity that is beyond our comprehension.

Dorothy Soelle writes, "Mysticism is . . . an experience of God, an experience of being one with God, an experience that God bestows on people." Even though we tend to doubt the authenticity of this type of unexpected prayer, we ought not to reject this gift. Mystical moments authenticate the amazing nearness and inexplicable immensity of God. When these gifts from the Spirit come to us, we cannot help but take notice. The best response to mystical moments is gratitude, not skeptical disbelief.

Many Ways to Pray

Mystical moments are the exception rather than the norm for prayer. There are a gazillion other ways to be in relationship with God. Henry C. Simmons and Jane Wilson refer to this in their book *Soulful Aging:*

Prayer is affirming God and oneself. Prayer is the whole person being attentive to God, longing for God, opening to God, reaching out to God, surrendering to God, needing God, centering oneself in God, communicating with God, offering oneself to God, resting in God. Prayer is the interiorizing of the Incarnation. Prayer is solitary and communal, personal and political. Prayer is profoundly immanent and profoundly transcendent; profoundly simple and profoundly mysterious. It is a knowing of God and a "not knowing." ... There is no place where prayer is impossible. There is no time when prayer is impossible. There is no way in which every person must pray.

Prayer is meant to be an uncomplicated gesture of love, although it is generally not perceived or presented in this manner. Professors and authors are apt to describe prayer as a decidedly complex process, one that sounds more like tedious work than it does a natural process of growing in a love-relationship. As Simmons and Wilson note, there really is no *best way* for every person to pray. Each of us must find and trust our own way. Each of us must also allow others to discover and claim their own way.

When a woman at a retreat in Florida stood up to speak, her message reflected this freedom of prayer. She explained how she spent the previous scheduled period of silence walking reflectively along a nearby river. She said that nature was where she felt her friendship with God was most nurtured and sustained. I guessed it took courage for her to share this conviction with the group because the majority of persons there were steeped in the time-honored, contemplative form known as "centering prayer." Fortunately, no one there tried to convince the creation-oriented retreatant that her way of praying was any less valuable than theirs.

One of the more challenging aspects of prayer is intercessory prayer. Jesus taught that we should ask for what we need and it will be given to us. ("For everyone who asks, receives; and the one who seeks, finds; and to the one who knocks, the door will be opened," Luke 11:10.) Does this mean that if we pray well enough, or long enough, we will get whatever we want? How do we pray for self and others without telling God what to do? In my estimation, no one has ever come up with a fully adequate answer to either question. What we do know in faith is that we *will* be given what we need for our journey — but it may not be what we want, demand, or expect.

When my dear cousin Theresa was terminally ill with cancer, several of her friends (who take the Bible too literally) assured her that if she had enough faith she would be cured. Theresa was an exceptionally faith-filled person but cancer still took her life. She did not receive the gift of a cure, but she did receive the spiritual gifts of an incredible inner strength and a tremendous ability to be graciously loving in spite of her continually dashed hopes and physical pain. The presence of God was so evident in her that even the hospital nurses who cared for Theresa in her final days wept when she died.

None of us can explain how God responds to intercessory prayer. We look for "evidence," but in the end we yield to

the Holy One with trust and confidence. Rather than convince God how our difficult situations ought to turn out, it
is more appropriate to give ourselves and others into God's
compassionate care. One of the beautiful prayers that a friend
of mine created is from the Gospel story of the woman who
touched the hem of Jesus' garment. When in pain or turmoil,
in need of guidance or care, my friend confidently touches
two fingers to the top of her thumb as a sign of holding on
to God with trust, just as the woman with the hemorrhage
reached out to touch the hem of Jesus' garment. Each of us
can reach out and touch the garment of God.

We can also pray by sitting with open hands, mentally placing in them anyone who is in need. This is an excellent prayer
for parents concerned about their child's well-being. The sym-
bol of open hands indicates the parents' willingness to not
cling too tightly to their child while, at the same time, giving the child lovingly into the protective care of the divine
Father/Mother.

Praying Our Life

Prayer can happen anywhere, anytime. Not only can we commune with God in church and in the solitude of our own
room but we can also do so in the midst of life's activities
whether in an office cubicle, a supermarket line, an airport ter-
minal, a laundry room, the bathroom, or bed. The content of
our prayer includes our individual talents, night dreams and
day dreams, physical, emotional, and psychological health,
varied relationships, memories, joys and sorrows, cultural,

geographical, and political landscapes, and much more. I did not believe any of this when I first learned how to pray. I thought prayer was meant to be one clean little corner and then there was the rest of my life. Not so.

We do not pray in a vacuum. Always prayer is to touch our life and life is to touch our prayer. Each part of who we are and how we are is what we bring to God. Our lived experience, no matter how commonplace or bizarre, is where our relationship with the divine evolves. Of course, there are always some pieces of our life that we'd definitely like to keep from God due to guilt, shame, pride, or an obsessive desire to be perfect. No part of who we are and how we are can be left out, however, because this is where we receive God's grace. Prayer ought never be separated and strained clean from what is happening in the rest of our life.

Our life experiences are where the Spirit teaches and nurtures us into greater wholeness. This is one reason why it is essential to be aware. Unless we are attuned to life within us and around us, we will miss countless opportunities of knowing how the Spirit is communicating with us. Instead of deleting the external world from our relationship with God, we are to enter it fully. Margaret Silf emphasizes this in her book, *Companions of Christ*:

Wherever and whoever God is for us, we will, and can only meet God where we are, in our embodied living, on our planet earth, in the living universe that enfolds our planet, and in the everyday world where we live and move and have our being. If we don't meet God in the everyday, we won't meet God at all.

Meeting God amid the everyday is evident in a story that Gregory Augustin Pierce tells about walking the floor one dark winter evening with one of his children who cried a lot at night. He is worried about trying to quiet the child so she will not awaken her twin sister. It is snowing outside and as he stands by the window with her, she stops crying, looks out the window and exclaims, "Snow!" Pierce is amazed. He wonders how the word "snow" came to this small girl who had not known the word before. At that moment, he is overcome with the gift of being a parent and rediscovers awe for the wonder of his child. In the word "snow," the Spirit moves him to see the power and beauty of his life as a parent and the deeper reality of the sacredness of his life.

In another situation, a woman (whom I will name "Lana") wrote to tell me about a significant dream she had after her young husband died of a heart attack. He left her with several little children and a challenging financial situation. In the dream Lana is walking through the living room and sees her husband sitting on the floor in front of his bookshelves. She runs to him, kneels down, and hugs him. As she feels the warmth of his arms, he seems utterly alive to her. Then Lana wakes up and realizes it is just a dream. She goes immediately to her husband's bookshelves and sits down by the place where he was in her dream. Amid her tears, there is a book on the shelf that is eye-level with her. When she pulls it out, she sees it is a book on grief. As it turns out, this is just the book she needs in order to start mending her lonely heart. In the following months, this book helped her move to a level of acceptance and peace as she mourned her husband's death.

We never know what commonplace part of our life may awaken us to God's presence and shift us toward a deeper place inside. Falling snow and night dreams are common events, but in the two situations just mentioned, they became sources for prayerful gratitude and healing from grief. In each case, the ordinariness of human nature serves to awaken human consciousness and provides a means of being drawn into closer union with God. Both Lana and Gregory's ordinary circumstances turned to "extra-ordinary" as they became mindful of the unseen presence moving in their midst. Each was given a touch of the Holy.

As we pray out of the ordinariness of our life, reflective pauses help clear our mind and heart so we can recognize how the Spirit moves among us. While morning is an excellent time to begin our day intentionally with God, the closing of the day invites us to reflect back over the hours we spent since getting out of bed. Celtic poet John O'Donohue writes:

> It is a valuable practice at night to spend a little while revisiting sanctuaries of your lived day. Each day is a secret story woven around the radiant heart of wonder. We let our days fall away like empty shells and miss all the treasures.

Again, there are many ways to meet God in the evening. Pope John Paul II suggested:

Put aside a little time in the evening especially for praying, for meditating, for reading a page of the Gospel or
an episode in the life of some saint. Create a zone of
desert and silence for yourself in that way.

For a long time I ignored evening prayer, not because I dis-
valued its worth but because tiredness enticed me to forego it.
Slowly I changed this habit. This last prayer of the day is never
long. I gather up gratitude for what went well since morning,
and express sorrow for any deliberately unloving acts. Often,
in this brief space of *looking back*, I am astounded at the inter-
weaving of God throughout the day's events. Always, now, I
close this evening prayer with entrusting my entire being into
the Holy One's care, peacefully remembering that divine light
and love fill my entire being.

Bleak Prayer

When we "pray our life" this includes the parts we wish were
not there. None of us wants pain of any kind, but we cannot always escape it. Because every experience of life touches
our relationship with God, we ought not be alarmed when
bleakness enters it. Our experience of prayer is influenced by
the condition of our body, mind, and spirit. If we are dealing
with woes of any type, we can expect our experience of prayer
to be affected. No one wants to feel empty and lifeless when
they pray, but sometimes our relationship with God appears
to be a vacant space of austere darkness. There will be days,

and maybe long stretches, when the experience of praying is mostly miserable, dreary, and undesirable.

Ann Weems wrote her powerful *Psalms of Lament* when she was grieving the homicide of her son, Todd. As in the Hebrew psalms, she cried out in rage and anguish, wailing over injustice and loss. Weems entered into her sorrow and brought the hollowness of her heart into her prayer. She did not deny her anger and heartache or try to cushion the blow of her pain with false sentiments of piety. Instead, Weems did as many in the scriptures before her — she voiced her hurt and trusted God to receive her wailing with the greatest tenderness. Weems encourages anyone feeling the immensity of loss to draw near to the Compassionate One and "in loud lament cry out the pain that lives in our souls."

Bleak times challenge us to continue to have faith that God will journey with us through the misery of the present situation, that no matter what the condition of our life circumstance, we will not give up on God. Macrina Wiederkehr's prayer in *A Tree Full of Angels* speaks to this trust:

> O Sustainer of Life...let me trust also the darkness of my own faith that is energized by my love. Even if my waiting in darkness were to be the only truth I ever taste, I would still believe.... The illumination that enables me to speak is found in waiting for you, my God. My tears and my love urge me to wait through the darkest of nights. So I will wait and never be without you.

There are times and situations when we are too weak and full of ache to cry out to God. This is particularly true when physical pain consumes every moment and we cannot muster the mental or emotional strength to focus on much of anything. When this happens, others can pray in our stead. I recall visiting an elderly sister from my community when she was in the hospital. She was deathly ill and could barely speak or move. Sister E. whispered her distress to me when I sat down beside her. She said a priest visitor had come in and when she expressed her concern about being unable to pray, he insisted, "You can too pray." I do not know what he meant, but his comment filled Sister E. with agonizing guilt. I assured her it was natural that she would not be able to think of a thing, not even to have strength to pray a rote prayer or the rosary. I suggested her prayer might be to surrender to the cross of illness that she was carrying, to trust that God knew her situation and the desire of her heart. I promised her that those of us who loved her would pray in her place. This promise seemed to bring her the peaceful resolution she needed.

There will be days, and maybe long stretches, when the experience of praying is mostly miserable, dreary, and undesirable.

Thomas Merton made the perceptive observation that when we think our prayer is the worst, it might actually be our best because when we are in a dismal state, we are unable to be our own "god." We are no longer deceived into thinking we are the ones in charge. When we are bent over with pain, all we can do is to throw ourselves into the divine arms, trusting we will receive compassion and strength to go on. During sieges of emptiness and dryness, instead of running away from what hurts and causes us trouble, we are wise to gather up our woe and head straight for the Holy One's embrace.

Praying the Eucharist

While each of the sacraments is an invitation to unite with the divine, the Eucharistic liturgy especially offers endless possibilities for communing with God. Certainly this is true at the time of receiving Communion. When I am lethargic or distracted this opportune time for prayer becomes routine and lacks reflective quality. The same is true for the rest of the Eucharistic liturgy. Because the Mass is a celebration filled with formal, rote prayers, they can become boringly familiar with repetition, causing our mind and heart to flee elsewhere. Eucharist can end up being anything but "prayer-full." It takes real effort to be attentive and responsive if we are to experience spiritual union with God through liturgical prayer.

Fortunately, there are always times when I am reawakened to the spiritual potency of the Eucharist in spite of my unawareness. One day when I held out my hands to receive Communion, there was no more Bread. I felt like a little bird with its mouth open, with nothing to be had. I stood and waited for what seemed an eternity until the Eucharistic minister returned with the remaining consecrated wafers. As I returned to my place, gratitude for the Gift I had received encompassed me.

Another day as I walked up to receive Communion, a little two- or three-year-old girl skipped up between the two aisles of communicants. She got to the front of the line and stood there with eyes wide open, looked up eagerly, and watched each of us who received. At that moment, I regained my own wonder for what was taking place.

Besides the act of receiving the Body of Christ, there are numerous other opportunities within the Eucharistic liturgy to move us into personal prayer. If we are open and vigilant, a thought from a good homily, the lines of a song, a text from the scripture readings, or a phrase from the Eucharistic prayer can draw us into a deepening sense of how God is moving within and among us. For example, the words to the Our Father hold immense potential for transforming prayer. Just one line such as "forgive us our trespasses as we forgive those who trespass against us" contains enough spiritual fuel to last a lifetime.

We never know when we might be moved to pray, to *really pray*, with the prayers of the Eucharist. A mother of two newly adopted foster children faced adjustment challenges due to the children's wounded past. She found surprising hope at the Eucharistic liturgy one day and wrote to tell me of the prayerful moment:

> I marvel at the gift that God has entrusted to us in all our kids. The second time our newest were with us at Mass, our oldest son and I were helping to lead music and my husband, our biological daughters, and our new daughter and son were in the front row. I looked up to see

them holding hands during the Our Father. It took them a while to get all linked up but it happened. I thought "that is how our relationship will be.... It will take a while but we will get linked up." The part shortly after that says "Lord, I am not worthy to receive you but only say the word and I shall be healed." For the only time in my life those words moved me. I was struck with how unworthy I am to receive the children (God is in them) and that healing can occur for them. Nothing is impossible for God.

Awareness of other people who gather for the Eucharist also lends possibilities for prayer. Stephen Fitzhenry, O.P., refers to this in his article "Qualities of a Contemplative Soul":

> And then there is the Eucharist: "Look beyond the bread you eat; look beyond the cup you drink." How obvious the gift is. Throughout history, souls have been nourished and mellowed by simply being in the presence of the Eucharistic Christ. They begin to understand how they can become Eucharistic people; allowing themselves to be taken by Jesus, blessed, broken, and distributed to others for their nourishment, passing on the gift, the wonder, and the grace of Christ.

Eucharist invites us to communicate with the Body of Christ in the consecrated bread/wine and it also connects us with the Eucharistic Christ in those who join with us for worship. Christ reaches out to us through each person who gathers for prayer. One time a teenage girl next to me hung her head and slumped back on the pew throughout the service. Her body language told me this was the last place she wanted to be. I wondered what caused her mood, perhaps a painful menstrual cycle, or a breakup with a young love, or alienation from a parent. I felt drawn to extend kindness and understanding to her. Throughout the liturgy, I deliberately united Christ's compassion to the young woman. I longed for her to be at peace. Eventually, I felt a gentle communion between myself and the unhappy teenager. This experience taught me the possibility of "passing on the gift, the wonder, and the grace of Christ" to others.

This is easy to do in the parish where I now participate in the Eucharistic liturgy. Each Sunday the pews fill with eager, devout immigrants. When I see dedicated families with beautiful children, and young, single men who have left family and friends to seek work, my heart opens wide to them. I think of the long, fearful journeys and struggles they endured to move away from their homeland and the image of the suffering, journeying Christ permeates my inner vision. Union with the divine comes easily as a sense of oneness with the Body of Christ rises within me. For I know that even though their stories are extremely different from mine, we are joined by our common faith and desire to be with our divine companion.

Keeping the Vigil of Mystery

Whether in the solitude of a chosen space of prayer, in the mundane or the marvelous moments of life, or in the gatherings of communal prayer, the Spirit draws us toward enduring love. Within the context of our life's diversity, we discover ways of praying that are the most beneficial for us to "catch the stirring of the Spirit." We squirm and wiggle less and less as the presence of divine love captivates our hearts. Almost without realizing it, we find ourselves leaning toward and listening to God with ever greater awareness and attentiveness.

"To keep the vigil of mystery" is to be like a sturdy oak tree waiting for the unrestrained wind to stir the far-reaching branches. Like the oak, we stand firmly rooted, grounded in the foundation of our relationship with God. We stand freely, the opened branches of our spirit like a sentinel ready for the slightest rustle of divine wisdom and guidance. We keep vigil, willingly and patiently. With each prayer we breathe, we trust the Holy One to stir in our heart and to hear the sighing of our soul.

Questions

1. When do you pray and how do you pray?

2. Which of the aspects described in this chapter most resonate with your experience and beliefs about prayer?

3. Have you experienced "unexpected prayer"? If so, what was this like?

4. With what do you most agree, or disagree, in this chapter?

Prayer

Nurturing Presence,
I turn the ears of my heart
in full attention to your voice.
I lean to catch the whispers
of your abiding love.
May I be ever and always open
to the countless places and times
you call me into relationship with you.
Amen.

Turning Prayer Inside Out

Great Traveler,
you beguile crestfallen disciples
on the road to Emmaus,
draw them in
with your arrowed questions,
urge them to turn the story
over, to recall each piece of it,
although you already know
the disturbing memory.

You speak your golden words,
softening the travelers' sadness,
revealing what their hearts (and mine),
yearn to believe: life thrives beyond death.

Slowly their sagging spirits rouse
with recognition, allured by the faint scent
of your prevailing presence.

"Stay! Stay! Stay with us!"
And you do.

You break bread with them,
and when the lamp of love

flames high, you rise
and gently slip away.

Joy erases past bewilderment,
propels the disciples
outward. They go, carrying a taste of love,
a voice of hope, a word of comfort
to those waiting in the wounded harbor
of disbelief.

Now, after the closeness of prayer,
I, too, go out, carrying the flaming heart
of communion, go to embrace
the Beloved
through the integrity of my life,

go to carry Love alight within me
out and beyond, into the heart of a world
where the same Lamp shines
for all to see.

— Joyce Rupp

Then they said to each other, "Were not our hearts burn-ing within us while he spoke to us on the way and opened the scriptures to us?" So they set out at once and returned to Jerusalem. (Luke 24:32–33a)

P RAYER IS MEANT to "grow us." Every divine encounter holds the possibility of transforming us. Genuine prayer is risky. It changes us, and we are never sure what those changes might be. We may not initially be aware of the alterations within ourselves because these movements are often imperceptible, but each authentic prayer brings our truest self a bit more to the surface of life. This transfor-mation includes discovering our preeminent virtues and our most dismal compulsions, our finest qualities and our most embarrassing traits.

The changes within us due to prayer are not just for our self. When we leave our place of prayer, the Spirit sends us forth to live as persons of great love. Our heart "knows" — has faith — that Someone greater than ourselves sends us on-ward. Like the two on the road to Emmaus, we go from meeting God in prayer to living in a way that attests to this encounter. As prayer slowly transforms us, we become trans-parent vessels of divinity. Our inherent goodness increasingly reflects divine love with greater generosity and authenticity.

The Spirit who led us inward to the secret depths of our heart now leads us outward to engage in life's pursuits. Like Jesus, we are led from the quiet places of personal prayer into the wider sphere of activity. Through each inner experience, the Spirit strengthens us in love and persuades us to carry this intertwining affection into the highways and byways of life. Like the two on the Emmaus road who were encircled in the aura of Christ's closeness, some part of us yearns to hang on to what we receive in prayer. But we cannot do so. We keep being nudged out of the nest of prayer to share what is maturing in us.

Even though our active involvement in the external ventures of life might give the appearance that we have left God behind in our place of prayer, this is not so. We move from the sacredness of personal prayer into the sacredness of daily life. Kathy Coffey expounds on this when she reflects on the Emmaus story in *Hidden Women of the Gospels:*

> Jesus' disclosure of himself to those who are "on the road" comes as good news to people who are often in motion. While some may criticize the frenzied mobility of our era, Jesus joins the journey. . . . The Emmaus revelation showed not only something about Jesus, but also something about us; that our most ordinary routines can be sacramental, . . . that our times and spaces are sacred.

The two disciples on the road pressed Jesus to stay and join them for a meal. He did so, breaking bread with them and kindling their hearts with renewed love. The disciples must have wanted to linger there forever, but Jesus sent them forth by disappearing from their sight. When this happened, the renewed disciples went out on the road again, turned back toward Jerusalem, taking with them their vibrant experience of the Risen Christ's presence. A parallel movement happens at the close of our prayer time. Like the two disciples heading outward, and in a manner similar to the final blessing of the Eucharistic liturgy, we go forth to bear God's love into every part and parcel of our day and night.

Carol Flinders observes this movement from personal prayer to the world at large in her work on the women mystics, *At the Root of This Longing*. Flinders comments on how much energy for good is elicited from the mystics' life with God: "When they had entered the deepest parts of themselves, the results were incredible: tremendous energy, stamina, resourcefulness, ease, wit, patience — and loving-kindness by the bucketful." The best of who we are comes alive when we give ourselves to God in prayer. As we enter the deeper part of ourselves, our potential for closeness with the Holy One and the resulting energy for service to others knows no bounds.

At the City Gates

The paradox of prayer is that as it strengthens us inwardly, it also strengthens us outwardly. As we grow spiritually, we become ever more effective catalysts of love in the marketplace. We discover the Holy One within us and the Holy One beyond us. We learn there are no divisions between the sacred and the secular when our vision is transformed. Our entire life becomes imbued with God-ness as we notice the Holy One's touch anywhere and everywhere.

Spiritual teachers in Buddhism say that after enlightenment one is to "enter the marketplace with helping hands." Christianity also insists that what we glean in our personal relationship with God we are to take into the rest of life. The perceptive English mystic Evelyn Underhill advises us to go up alone to the mountain and come back as an ambassador to the world. Scripture likewise encourages us to discover God in the stream of life's activity.

The Book of Proverbs offers striking testimony to this by presenting the image of divine Wisdom sitting at the city gates. Wisdom does not just sit there; she calls out to be heard amid the flurry of the city's business: "Wisdom cries out in the street; in the open squares she raises her voice. Down the crowded ways she calls out; at the city gates she utters her words.... Lo, I will pour out to you my spirit, I will acquaint you with my words" (Prov. 1:20–21, 23b). Later, in chapter 8, this theme is repeated: "Does not Wisdom call, and Understanding raise her voice? On top of the heights along the road, at the crossroads she takes her stand; By the gates at the approaches to the city, in the entryways she cries aloud" (Prov. 8:1:3).

In biblical times, the "gates of the city" were the entrance through which all residents and visitors passed. One can imagine the hustle and bustle of these comings and goings in the *crowded* streets, much like the constant activity pervading our own modern lives. The city gates symbolize the place where the Holy One can be found. While we listen and watch for divine Wisdom at the door of our personal prayer, we also listen and watch at the door of all that happens in the rest of life. Whatever and whoever is part of our daily journeying, there Holy Wisdom waits at the threshold of those experiences.

God is to be found especially at the *city gates* of our work. When Gregory Pierce writes about the spiritual nature of employment in *Spirituality @ Work,* he queries: "Why would we want to look for God in our work?" Pierce then goes on to suggest: "Most of us spend so much of our time working that it would be a shame if we couldn't find God there. A more complex reason is that there is a creative energy in work that is somehow tied to God's creative energy. If we can understand and enter into that connection, perhaps we can use it to transform the workplace into something quite remarkable."

As Pierce notes, work itself is to be a source of transformation. In order for this to occur, we need a healthy prayer life to influence how we approach and carry out whatever we do for our livelihood. John O'Donohue describes this process in *Anam Cara:* "When we perform an action, the invisible within us finds a form, and comes to expression. Therefore, our work should be the place where the soul can enjoy becoming visible and present. The rich unknown, reserved and precious within us, can emerge into visible form."

When we maintain and nourish our relationship with God, our Christlike qualities will be evident in the way we go about making a living at the "city gate" of our work. When our prayer "grows us," sometimes the way we make a living also grows and changes. Work that gorges on our every waking hour with no time left for loved ones or for a development of inner life, work that presses us into dishonesty or deceit, work that contributes to a lack of self-worth, or work that pushes us into actions that beget violence and endanger others, is not compatible with the Christlike qualities evolving from prayer.

Besides being at the "city gates" of our jobs, God is in the entanglements and disturbances, in the tumbles and turns that rankle us. Few of us welcome interruptions in our carefully crafted plans, yet this is also where Holy Wisdom reveals meaning and offers crucial opportunity for spiritual growth. God provides both guidance and challenge for the transformation of self and the world through the very people and situations who show up unannounced or unwelcome "at the crossroads" of our life.

Caryll Houselander, an English artist and writer of the mid-1900s, is a prime example of meeting and being transformed by those who come through the "city gates" of her world. She had an amazing ability to heal emotionally and mentally disabled persons by the sheer gift of her love. Houselander writes in *The Reed of God:*

> If we look for Christ only in the saints, we shall miss Him. If we look for Him only in those people who seem to have the sort of character we personally consider to be Christian, that which we call our "ideal," we shall miss the whole meaning of His abiding in us....
>
> Our search through faith and courage and love is a great going out into the darkness, a reaching out to others in darkness, believing that Christ is there in each one; but not in the way that we expect, not in the way that we think He should be, not in the way that we

already understand, but in the way that He chooses to be, Who is Himself the Way.

The Compassion of Jesus

If prayer is to assist us in welcoming the Christ in disguise and enabling us to develop Christlike qualities, then compassion will certainly be one of the central virtues growing and maturing in us as our prayer life grows and matures. The central quality of Jesus weaving through his teachings and activity is that of compassion. He not only instructs his followers about the basic tenets of this central gospel virtue; Jesus clothes himself with compassion in both his attitude and actions. Time and again we see how compassionate Jesus is. He empathizes with those who grieve. He does all he can to help the ill and disabled. He wants to be sure the hungry are fed, leads the wayward back to their best selves, speaks of justice for the poor, accepts disciples whose foibles challenge his patience, and forgives his enemies rather than being retaliatory.

The abundant compassion of Jesus is closely linked to his own experience of prayer. The Gospels tell us that Jesus withdrew to be alone with the Holy One. No one knows what took place in these sacred hours, but surely the solitude and silence of those "deserted places" must have restored his human depletion of compassion (Luke 5:16). After leaving these periods of prayer, Jesus was immediately jostled back into a life requiring immense amounts of love, which he continued to share unwaveringly (Mark 1:35–39).

The compassion that Jesus lives and teaches is based on the reality of our inter-relatedness with one another. Jesus compares himself to a vine and us to the branches, indicating that we are united with divinity much like life surging through the vine or energy flowing through the body (John 15:1–6). Not only that, Jesus maintains that whatever we do to one another, we do to him — to the Holy One. When Jesus encourages others to extend kindness and empathy, he tells them: "Whoever receives you, receives me, and whoever receives me receives the one who sent me" (Matt. 10:40). In the well-known teaching recorded in Matthew 25:31–46, Jesus speaks of the hungry, the thirsty, the stranger, the naked, and the imprisoned, saying that anyone who has extended kindness to them has done so to him. He concludes the lesson with: "Amen, I say to you, whatever you did not do for one of these least ones, you did not do for me."

From these teachings evolved the theology of the Body of Christ described in 1 Corinthians 12:12–27, an insightful passage suggesting that whatever affects one of us affects the entire group:

> As a body is one though it has many parts, and all the parts of the body, though many, are one body, so also Christ.... Now the body is not a single part, but many. If a foot would say, "Because I am not a hand, I do not belong to the body" it does not for this reason belong any less to the body. And if the ear would say, "Because I am not an eye I do not belong to the body," it does not for this reason belong any less to the body.... The

eye cannot say to the hand, "I do not need you.... If one part suffers, all the parts suffer with it; if one part is honored, all the parts share its joy. Now you are Christ's body, and individually parts of it.

I have noted earlier that we do not come to prayer alone. Always God is with us. Now it becomes clear that we also have with us the world community. Edwina Gateley remarked, "God is the Great Illegal Immigrant," implying that each person is a sanctuary of the divine, including the poor and the unacceptable. All of us are united as in a sacred web of Love. We bring humanity with us into our prayer. We meet humanity again when we move out of our prayer and step into the vast world of diversity. Truly, we are not alone when we come to prayer.

Breathing Compassion

Jack Kornfield writes that "the truly loving person breathes in the pain of the world and breathes out compassion." As we become more loving due to prayer, we begin to breathe as Kornfield suggests. There is a story told of Mahatma Gandhi getting on a train just as the train starts to pull out. As he jumps onto the train, one of his sandals falls off onto the tracks. Gandhi quickly slips off the other sandal and lets it fall onto the tracks, too. Someone near him asks, "Why did you do that?" Gandhi replies, "Now someone will have a pair of shoes to wear."

How I wish I had that much compassion. My first thought would be about my unshod foot. Gandhi's was of the larger world, of those who could not afford a pair of shoes for their calloused, cracked feet. Gandhi was intrinsically bound to the vaster world of those who needed the basic necessities of life. Gandhi was not a Christian, although he had a great respect for Christianity. He was faithful to his own daily Hindu meditation, and it shows in his compassionate stance. Gandhi's prayer was turned inside out. We can do the same with ours. Jesus has shown us the way.

One of the foundations of compassion is the requirement to have an open, non-judgmental heart. ("Stop judging and you will not be judged. Stop condemning and you will not be condemned. Forgive and you will be forgiven," Luke 6:37.) Non-judgment is a tough virtue to acquire and practice. Marc Ian Barasch, author of *Field Notes on the Compassionate Life,* observes how our minds easily take off on the pervasive action of judging others when doing something so common as walking through a shopping mall:

> My finicky responses to the goods on display merge with my reactions to the people I pass — little covetous twinges, subtle flickers of attitude, petty judgments on how people walk, talk, dress, and chew gum.

If I continually compare others to my standard of life and behavior and expect them to act accordingly, I will fail to respond compassionately. I will deny the spiritual interdependence between us and act on the belief that our lives have no connection with one another. At most, I will offer self-pity, which is a form of seeing myself as separate from, and superior to, the other person. If my daily prayer is allowing for steady purification of my false judgments and ego-orientation, the kindness that God's Spirit stirs in my heart will flow over into my daily actions. I will move *toward*, not away from, those whose lives plead for a touch of understanding and consolation. Then, the Christ-quality of compassion will wrap its tender arms around all that I am and do.

When I remember that God tolerates and forgives the smelliness of my own faults and failings, I am more ready to accept what I find disdainful in others.

The life and actions of Jesus show that compassion requires more than a comfortable feeling of empathy and concern, that compassion is more than a cozy choice of good will toward someone in need. I know I have a lot of praying yet to do before I pass beyond my natural inclinations to judge others according to my standards and preferences. I continue to be challenged to go beyond my prejudices and self-centeredness, to be generous with my kindness and acceptance. I often fail at doing so when certain people or situations do not appeal to me.

Such was the day I drove away after the Eucharistic liturgy and stopped to buy a greeting card at the local drugstore. As I walked down the aisle, I saw ahead of me a stooped, disheveled man who was probably homeless. The stench coming from him was horrific. I looked to see that he had wet himself, and probably more than that, given the repulsive smell. Instead of continuing on toward him, I turned around and hurried down another aisle, trying to avoid him at all costs. I completely forgot the teaching on the Body of Christ — that what I was doing to this man, I was doing to the Holy One. Not only that, I lost all sense of having just received the Eucharist, whose Christ-love is meant to draw me nearer to others, not push them away.

When I experience God's non-judgmental and loving acceptance of myself in prayer, I am called to extend these same identifying features of compassion to others. When I remember that God tolerates and forgives the *smelliness* of my own faults and failings, I am more ready to accept what I find disdainful in others. The more I know my own great need for the embrace of a merciful, forgiving God, the more I can be forgiving and merciful to those who wound me. The more I truly believe the Holy One loves and accepts me as I am, while longing for me to be all I can be, the more I will gather to my heart all who are part of this vast world of ours.

St. Paul recognized this ability to share compassion when he wrote to the Corinthians: "Blessed be the God...the Father of compassion and God of all encouragement, who encourages us in our every affliction, so that we may be able to encourage those who are in any affliction with the encouragement with which we ourselves are encouraged by God" (2 Cor. 1:3–4): When we suffer and receive God's caring love through others, our own compassion is warmed and readied to be extended to others.

Some of the most compassionate and caring people are those whose lives have wobbled on the deadly edges of Job-like difficulties. Amid these challenging afflictions and distressful encounters, suffering people learn the depth of their resiliency and the extent of their courage. They discover, too, the power of prayer and the unfailing strength of God's enduring grace. When they emerge out of these encounters of pain and struggle, those who have suffered often extend to others the same great love that brought them out of the caverns of their own desolation.

After we have gone through a time of suffering, we eventually come to know and understand how compassion was birthed in our times of prayer. We may have thought "nothing was happening" because suffering overtook us so utterly, but grace was at work, gestating loving-kindness in us. When the opportunity presents itself, this compassion arises and is reflected in our thoughts, words, and deeds.

Did You Love Well?

Mustering up magnanimous thoughts of compassion at a distance is relatively easy. Talking passionately about being a person of love takes little effort. Compassion entails more than pleasant words spoken to God or meditating on scripture texts. True compassion necessitates our moving beyond self. It demands our vulnerability, stepping out of our comfort zone, giving up our precious time and sacrosanct schedule.

"To offer the heart is not like offering a fingernail or a lock of hair we were ready to discard anyway, it is to offer the core, the most essential part of our being," comments Sharon Salzberg.

Evelyn Underhill spoke and wrote astutely about prayer and the Christian life. In *The House of the Soul*, she refers to the outcome of prayer and our life with God:

> "When the evening of this life comes," says St. John of the Cross, "you will be judged on love." The only question asked about the soul's... gifts that were made to it, will be: "Have you loved well?..." Was everything that was done, done for love's sake? Were all the doors opened, that the warmth of Charity might fill the whole house; the windows cleaned, that they might more and more radiate from within its mysterious divine light? Is the separate life of the [soul's] house more and more merged in the mighty current of the city's life?

The surest sign of prayer's genuineness is when it influences what we say and do. To love well we need inspiration, motivation, dedication, and commitment. These gifts are elicited in healthy prayer that encourages risk-taking and shapes our loving actions. I have witnessed this reality time and again in those I companion as a spiritual director. There is one man, in particular, who exemplifies how prayer changes us into people who love well. His good acts have evolved through years of faithful commitment to daily prayer. As with many deeds of love, he is often unaware of their influence, but on one occasion, he received assurance of their power to bless another.

One morning when we met to reflect on his life with God, this man (whom I will call "Tony") told me about a friend of his who was dying. They had worked together at a factory years ago before it closed. When Tony learned his friend was in a hospice home, he decided to visit him. The thought came to Tony that he could invite some other men to visit who had also worked with his dying friend. Tony said he hesitated doing so, wondering if his male friends would be okay with openly expressing compassion and concern. Although Tony was not sure of their comfort level with a dying person, he went ahead, took the chance, and gathered the old friends together.

When they first arrived, the men hesitated outside the hospice room, unsure of what to say or how to act, but Tony said once they were all in the room together, an amazing thing took place. They held the dying man's hand, offered words of care and comfort, and let their tears come. In Tony's words: "They expressed and demonstrated compassion equal to any I've ever seen. The patient and his family were incredibly grateful." Afterward, the patient's wife told Tony, "It is obvious to me that God has intervened to bring you all here today. Nothing could've been more important to him than a visit by people from the factory." The patient's oldest son added, "Dad was grinning the whole time and he hasn't smiled for six weeks."

This is the "difference" Kenneth Leech speaks of when he defines prayer as a relationship with God that is intended to "make a difference." Yes, prayer can make a difference, not only in our own life, but in the lives of those whom our presence touches. All we need do is rise from our prayer and choose to share the love that the Spirit quietly sparks in us.

These acts of love are usually not huge ones. More frequently they are quite small. But that is how most acts of love change the world — one small kindness after another is generated from the fruits of prayer. Mother Teresa and her sisters are a prime example of this. So is a Vietnamese woman named Chan Khong and the people who lived in her neighborhood. When she was fourteen years old, Chan wanted to do something for the poor children in the slums of Vietnam. She went to her neighbors and asked each of them to give her just three handfuls of rice a day for the children in the streets.

Prayer is never done. Our growing is never finished. The giving of our goodness is never completed. Our journey with the Holy One goes on and on.

After some time, she then began also asking for ten cents a day from these same generous people. Seven years later, at age twenty-one, Chan Khong joined their work with the Vietnamese meditation master Thich Nhat Hanh. Eventually there were ten thousand people working in the program to help the poor, thanks to the daily "small" gifts of her neighbors and herself. When Chan Khong was telling her story to a journalist, she said: "Do not despise the small act. Every small act, if you do it deeply, profoundly, can touch the whole universe."

A *deep and profound* act of kindness springs from the river of love in our soul. This river flows in and out of dedicated prayer. The fruits of our union with God can be measured only by the amount of love that pours forth from us into the world. If we want to know how our prayer is influencing our life with God, we can ask: "How non-judgmental, generous, compassionate, patient, forgiving, humble, justice-oriented, and selfless am I?" These are some of the key markers of healthy prayer. They are also some of the most challenging virtues to live. Dorothee Soelle explains it this way:

> The question which is often put to me, "Do you be-lieve in God?," usually seems a superficial one. If it only means that there is an extra place in your head where God sits, then God is in no way an event which changes your whole life, an event from which, as Buber says of real revelation, I do not emerge unchanged. We should really ask, "Do you live out God?" That would be in keeping with the reality of the experience.

Our mustard-seed actions of care and kindness are our way of "living out God." Steadfast, daily prayer can do so much. One deed to bring about justice holds great power. One effort to "be there" for another can alter a day, or a life, forever. Dorothy Day, founder of the Catholic Worker movement, held firmly to this belief as a foundation of her work. She said, "We can throw our pebble in the pond and be confident that its ever widening circle will reach around the world." That is how extensive one little pebble of prayer and action is. It only takes one person with a heart full of love and a desire to alleviate suffering to make a significant difference in the larger sphere of humankind.

Noisy Contemplation

Some years ago, I read an article by William Callahan in which he described a form of prayer in the marketplace called "noisy contemplation." Callahan pointed out that to contemplate means to "look lovingly." He emphasized that it does not take much effort to pray in the context of busyness. We can all do it. One way is by casting a non-judgmental, loving gaze upon every person we meet. (Some spiritual teachers describe this gaze as "looking with soft eyes.") Callahan advised his readers to first extend this loving gaze toward those who have a special place in one's heart. Then, to progressively behold colleagues, and, finally, strangers, with this same kind look.

Joanna Macy, a teacher of social action, offers a similar suggestion: "Look at the next person you see. It may be a lover, child, co-worker, bus driver, or your own face in the mirror. Regard him or her with the recognition that in this person are gifts for the healing of our world. In him/her are powers that can redound to the joy of all beings." I began practicing this form of prayer after I read Callahan and Macy's ideas and have done so ever since. It works. And it takes so little effort once one becomes aware of looking kindly instead of staring numbly, or harshly, at others.

A friend of mine told me how she, too, practices "noisy contemplation" in her profession now. She shared a story of her early years of nursing when she was overcome with the intensity and amount of medical care her patients required. There never seemed to be enough time to give each one the attention they needed and deserved. One day my friend was driving home from work, exhausted from long hours of endless demands. She reflected on her day and came to the conclusion that she did all the right things a nurse was expected to do, but not once had she ever really looked at any of the people she was helping. Instead, she went about like an automaton from room to room, paying little attention to any of the patients as persons. Tears of sadness flowed at this realization, and my friend resolved from that day onward to deliberately behold each patient with reverence.

The quality of our presence is what counts in the larger sphere of life. Our thoughts, words, and actions can become beautiful icons of the Beloved's benevolence. This love is nurtured in times of prayer and shows in our work and life-events. St. Paul wrote to Timothy: "I remind you to stir into flame the gift of God that you have...(2 Tim. 1:6). We kindle the gifts given in prayer when we allow the flame of love to shine in our life.

Striking the match of care and kindness takes a little effort. A woman on staff at a retreat center confided her experience of this as we spoke over dinner one evening. She described a

troubled man who often came to the center. He was bother-
some and both the staff and retreatants did their best to avoid
him. She felt badly about this and, in her words, "I tried to
be kind to him and let him know I cared." One day the man
said to her, "Whenever I am with you, even for a brief time,
I see the loving presence of God in you." She was astounded
and had no idea that the glow of kindness in her was giving
hope to him. All it took was a bit of effort on her part to
reach out with care.

Disciples of love are always growing in their efforts to follow Christ. Daily prayer sustains and enlivens love in their
hearts. Although they stumble, trip over their misdeeds, and
lose the way to love, prayer helps them start over again. Disciples of love continually return to silence and solitude in order
to fan the flame of devotion and foster their ability to follow
in the Teacher's ways. When we take the risk to pray, we open
ourselves to being changed into these disciples of love.

Spiritual Transformation

"I don't think I can ever be transformed," blurted out a
woman who came regularly for spiritual direction. I appreci-
ated her honesty but her comment surprised me. Upon further
listening, I discovered that she considered "spiritual transformation" too noble an undertaking and far beyond her reach.
I encouraged her to review the choices she made each day and
to note how they were changing her into a Christlike person.
In doing so, she would see her journey of transformation.
With this guidance, she then recognized the growth in her life

as a dedicated minister, a faithful spouse, a loving mother, a daily meditator, and a person strongly committed to global justice issues. She was truly being changed into love, day by day, but she had allowed the seeming hugeness of the process to scare her into thinking transformation was not possible for her.

Perhaps the disciples also questioned whether they could be spiritually transformed when the Risen Christ sent them forth with the mandate: "Go into the whole world and proclaim the gospel to every creature" (Mark 16:15). Jesus had given them similar instructions during his public ministry when he sent these disciples ahead of him, "in pairs to every town and place he intended to visit. He said to them, '...Carry no money bag, no sack, no sandals'" (Luke 10:1, 4a). By urging the disciples to live simply, Jesus was advising them to stay focused on the true purpose of their journey and not get distracted or preoccupied with anything but the gospel message. He was saying in effect, "Remember all I have taught you about kindness, non-judgment, compassion, forgiveness, and justice for all. Go, be a person of great love. Teach this love not only by what you say but by how you live."

Living as a person of great love is, of course, a daunting challenge. Becoming more Christlike entails a sometimes tedious and slow process. Let us not give in to self-doubt when there is seemingly little to show for our desire to be transformed into love. No matter how poor we may feel inside, there is always something to give. The well of divine love in us never goes dry. The spiritual sustenance from this well fills our hearts and contains the goodness we share as we go forth to employ our gifts for the transformation of the world.

Transformation is not always a pleasant process. The journey of prayer is sometimes troubling, challenging, and relentless as the Spirit pursues us with the call to be the person we are meant to be. Through daily communication with God, our ability to bring the love of Christ in our hearts into every arena of life is strengthened and re-energized. Because of what happens in our prayer, we can lead the kind of purposeful life that Linda McNamar describes:

> Developing a sense of personal purpose and being true to our core values allows us to see our lives in a larger context.... In living a purposeful life, we recognize that our career is more than just working for a paycheck, and our relationships are more than just being together. There is something of value for us to contribute and to learn in every situation. Each day is a new beginning in our chosen work, and each day we can be renewed even in the most trying relationships. Every day we can ask ourselves if we are living according to our highest purpose, right where we find ourselves. The answer to that question will tell us whether to stay or go. Vision and purpose don't come from what we are doing, but from how we are doing it. Spirit's grandness can be expressed through us in every situation.

How we approach God, life, and prayer makes all the difference. Not long ago I received a letter from a reader about one of my publications. She commented, "You confess to being less than perfect, to having doubts, to saying unkind things, and to enduring periods of darkness in the soul. In your willingness to open yourself up to public scrutiny you have enabled me to look within myself with more patience, more forgiveness, and less condemnation. . . . I just had my seventy-first birthday. . . . I'm still learning, still growing, and it just gets better all the time." I love that letter, not so much for the personal affirmation it extends to me, but for her enthusiastic acceptance of her continually unfolding relationship with God. Prayer is never done. Our growing is never finished. The giving of our goodness is never completed. Our journey with the Holy One goes on and on.

When Benedictine monk Bede Griffiths was teaching about meditation and life, he asked: "What can we do?" He supplied an answer, saying, "We can become a sign. Whatever happens, become a sign of divine joy and a fountain of divine love." Griffiths knew by his own experience that the purpose of prayer is ultimately to bring forth and share the kind of love that shines with divine radiance.

Going Forth as Catalysts of Goodness

Whether we feel it or not, whether we allow ourselves to believe it or not, the potential for us to be catalysts of goodness is real and possible. Prayer is one of the key places where the Spirit activates this metamorphosis of our hearts into a quality of love reflective of divinity. As we continue to unite with the Beloved, we grow in our ability to be conveyers of this love and light. Our individual qualities and giftedness (our goodness, our God-ness) shines forth. As disciples of love, we go forth to share our generous self-giving acts of kindness. We go to those whose life begs our voice of justice and our heart of compassion.

We are like the persons in scripture who are told to "get up" and go forth. Numerous prophets were called to get up and carry God's message to those in need of some sort of change in their life. Joseph hears the call to "go" in a dream: "Get up. Take Mary and the child into Egypt." Jesus tells those who are healed to "get up" and live a spiritually renewed life. In chapter 8 of the Acts of the Apostles, Philip "got up and set out" after the angel of God gave him the message to do so. Philip does not know why he is going forth until he comes to the Ethiopian who is struggling to understand Christ's message. After Philip explains the meaning to him, the Ethiopian asks to be baptized. All this happened because Philip "got up and set out" when he sensed the call to "go forth."

Every day the Spirit encourages us to go forth from our prayer and take some action for the benefit of both self and humanity. The more we remain faithful to our relationship with the Holy One, the more energized and inspired we will be to let this love permeate all we are and do. In spite of our inherent incompleteness and the painful events that come our way, the wonder of life will unmask itself and astound us with its beauty and sacredness. Through faithfulness to daily prayer, union with God will continue to deepen and strengthen. Each day our prayer will be turned inside out as we venture out to live as a person of great love.

Questions

1. How has prayer changed you?

2. What aspect of your life particularly challenges you to live compassionately?

3. When were you called to "go forth" and what was this like for you?

4. With what do you most agree, or disagree, in this chapter?

Prayer

> Great Teacher,
> you draw me to your heart.
> You reach me with your love.
> You inspire me with your message,
> and then you send me out to others.
> May I love well.
> As I go forth from my prayer,
> may I reflect the radiance of your goodness.
> Amen.

Conclusion

A Kernel of Corn
and a Little Teapot

T HERE IS NO END to what could be written about
prayer, but everything can be succinctly summed up in
a poem by Rabindranath Tagore and a story by Dr. Rachel
Naomi Remen.

In Tagore's striking poem, a beggar stands waiting for alms.
Along comes the Holy One disguised as a person of royalty
dressed in rich robes and riding a fine horse. This regal dignitary stops in front of the beggar whose heart leaps with joy
in anticipation of a big contribution. To the beggar's great
dismay, instead of giving something, the bejeweled personage
asks the beggar: "And what do you have to give me?" The
disappointed beggar is put off by this unseemly request. He
reaches into his tattered sack of belongings and pulls out one
kernel of corn which he gives to the dignitary. At the end of
the day, this same royal figure returns, comes to where the
beggar is sitting, leans over, and places one kernel of gold in
the beggar's outstretched hand. As the person of royalty rides
away, the beggar weeps with regret, saying, "How I wished I
had the heart to give You my all."

In my own life, I am often the beggar reaching in for the one kernel of corn, but once in a while, my heart enlarges enough to present my entire life to the Beloved. In spite of the countless times I have held back and given much less than was asked from my love, I find a long list of gifts spilling over from my journey of prayer. Thanks to God's generosity I have received much more than one little kernel of gold. These blessings include: a certain serenity amid life's continuous ups and downs, direction and guidance, perspective on life and fuller meaning, energizing encouragement and hope, an unmasking of my illusions, awareness of inner goodness and challenges to share the best of who I am, recognition of life as a daily gift, and a deep sense of kinship with all that exists.

Life is everywhere, hidden in the most ordinary and unlikely places. . . . All it needs is your faithfulness.

And now for the story. In *My Grandfather's Blessings*, Rachel Naomi Remen tells of an endearing grandfather who brought presents when he came to visit her. One day, when she was four years old and living on the sixth floor of an apartment building in New York City, he came with a little paper cup filled with dirt. They went into the nursery together where he found a teapot from her dollhouse set. Her grandfather filled the teapot with water and showed her how to put a few drops of water in the cup, saying: "If you promise to put some water in it every day, you may see something happen." She promised her grandfather she would do this, and then he placed the cup of dirt on the windowsill.

At first, the little girl was interested in seeing what might happen, but as the days went by and nothing changed in the cup of dirt, she found it harder and harder to put water in it. After a week she asked her grandfather if it was time to stop. He told her "no" and added reassuringly, "Keep watering it every day." The second week was even more difficult for the little girl to put water in the cup, and she started to resent it. She even tried to return the cup to her grandfather. He simply smiled and said, "Every day, every day." By the third week, she sometimes forgot and would have to get out of bed at night to do the watering, but she never missed a single day. Each time she told her grandfather that she wanted to stop, he smiled lovingly and encouraged her with the same words, "Every day."

One morning when she went to put water in the cup, she was astonished to see two little green leaves above the dirt. Each day the leaves grew bigger. She could not wait to tell her grandfather about the wondrous thing that had happened. When he came to visit, he shared her joy at the green leaves and explained to her, "Life is everywhere, hidden in the most ordinary and unlikely places." She was delighted and asked him, "And all it needs is water?" Gently, her grandfather touched her on the top of her head and said, "No, all it needs is your faithfulness."

Like this young child who watered the seemingly dead soil in the little cup, we must be willing to faithfully tend our

God-relationship each day so it can grow. There will be times when we, too, forget to do the watering, times when we may even resist or resent the practice of prayer, times when we doubt the worth of it, but we keep on "watering," anyhow. As we do so, we renew our trust that little leaves of spiritual growth are sprouting from our daily communication with the beloved companion of our soul.

Like the beggar by the roadside, God requests our generous love. Like the child watering the seeds, God asks our faithfulness. Bring these two gifts to prayer every day and God will do the rest.

Bibliography

Because the number of publications on prayer and related topics is vast, I have chosen to list only the resources that are cited in this book.

Ainsworth, Percy. *The Pilgrim Church*. London: Robert Culley Publishing, 1909.

Arrien, Angeles. *The Four-Fold Way: Walking the Paths of the Warrior, Teacher, Healer and Visionary*. San Francisco: HarperSanFrancisco, 1993.

Barasch, Marc Ian. *Field Notes on the Compassionate Life: A Search for the Soul of Kindness*. Emmaus, PA: Rodale, 2005.

Barks, Coleman, and Michael Green. *The Illuminated Prayer: The Five Times Prayer of the Sufis*. New York: Ballantine, 2000.

Coffey, Kathy. *Hidden Women of the Gospels*. Maryknoll, NY: Orbis Books, 2003.

D'Arcy, Paula. *Sacred Threshold: Crossing the Inner Barrier to a Deeper Love*. New York: Crossroad, 2004.

Edwards, Denis. *Breath of Life: A Theology of the Creator Spirit*. Maryknoll, NY: Orbis Books, 2004.

Finley, James. *Merton's Palace of Nowhere: A Search for God through Awareness of the True Self*. Notre Dame, IN: Ave Maria Press, 1978.

Flinders, Carol Lee. *At the Root of This Longing*. San Francisco: HarperSanFrancisco, 1998.

Gateley, Edwina. *A Mystical Heart: 52 Weeks in the Presence of God*. New York: Crossroad, 1998.

Griffiths, Bede. *Bede Griffiths: Essential Writings*. Selected with introduction by Thomas Matus. Maryknoll, NY: Orbis Books, 2004.

Harvey, Andrew. *The Way of Passion: A Celebration of Rumi*. Berkeley, CA: Frog, Ltd., 1984.

Hillesum, Etty. *An Interrupted Life: The Diaries of Etty Hillesum 1941–1943*. New York: Washington Square Press, 1985.

Houselander, Caryll. *The Reed of God*. Notre Dame, IN: Ave Maria Press, 2006.

Johnson, Elizabeth A. *She Who Is: The Mystery of God in Feminist Theological Discourse*. New York: Crossroad, 1993.

Kornfield, Jack. *A Path with Heart: A Guide through the Perils and Promises of the Spiritual Life*. New York: Bantam Books, 1993.

Leech, Kenneth. *True Prayer: An Introduction to Christian Spirituality*. London: Sheldon Press, 1980.

Macy, Joanna. *World as Lover, World as Self*. Berkeley, CA: Parallax Press, 1991.

Markova, Dawna. *I Will Not Die an Unlived Life: Reclaiming Purpose and Passion*. Berkeley, CA: Conari Press, 2000.

May, Gerald. *The Dark Night of the Soul*. San Francisco: HarperSanFrancisco, 2004.

McGinn, Bernard. *Meister Eckhart: Teacher and Preacher*. Mahwah, NJ: Paulist Press, 1986.

Merton, Thomas. *New Seeds of Contemplation*. Norfolk, CT: New Directions, 1961.

Nouwen, Henri. *With Open Hands*. Notre Dame, IN: Ave Maria Press, 1972.

O'Donohue, John. *Anam Cara: Spiritual Wisdom from the Celtic World*. New York: Bantam Press, 1997.

Pierce, Gregory F. A. *Spirituality @ Work: Ten Ways to Balance Your Life On-the-Job*. Chicago: Loyola Press, 2001.

Powers, Jessica. "To Live with the Spirit" from *The House at Rest*. Pewaukee, WI: Carmelite Monastery, 1984.

Rahner, Karl. *Karl Rahner: Spiritual Writings*. Edited by Philip Endean. Maryknoll, NY: Orbis Books, 2004.

Reeves, Nancy. *I'd Say "Yes" God, If I Knew What You Wanted*. Kelowna, BC: Northstone, 2001.

Remen, Rachel Naomi. *My Grandfather's Blessings*. New York: Riverhead, 2000.

Richardson, Jan L. *Night Visions: Searching the Shadows of Advent and Christmas*. Cleveland: United Church Press, 1998.

Salzberg, Sharon. *Loving-Kindness: The Revolutionary Art of Happiness*. Boston: Shambhala, 1995.

Silf, Margaret. *Companions of Christ: Ignatian Spirituality for Everyday Living*. Grand Rapids, MI: William B. Eerdmans, 2005.

Simmons, Henry C., and Jane Wilson. *Soulful Aging: Ministry through the Stages of Adulthood.* Macon, GA: Smyth & Helwys Publishing, 2001.

Soelle, Dorothee. *Dorothee Soelle: Essential Writings.* Selected with an introduction by Dianne L. Oliver. Maryknoll, NY: Orbis Books, 2006.

St. Teresa of Avila: The Collected Works. Vol. 1. Trans. Kieran Kavanaugh and Otilio Rodriguez. Washington, DC: ISC Publishing, 1976.

Tagore, Rabindranath. *The Gitanjali.* New York: Macmillan, 1913.

Underhill, Evelyn. *Evelyn Underhill: Essential Writings,* Selected with an introduction by Emilie Griffin. Maryknoll, NY: Orbis Books, 2003.

Weems, Ann. *Psalms of Lament.* Louisville: Westminster/John Knox Press, 1995.

Wiederkehr, Macrina. *A Tree Full of Angels: Seeking the Holy in the Ordinary.* New York: Harper & Row, 1988.

"Truly a spirituality for the 21st century!"
— Dolores Leckey

Catholic Spirituality for Adults

General Editor
Michael Leach

Forthcoming volumes include:

- *Holiness* by William O'Malley
- *Diversity of Vocations* by Marie Dennis
- *Charity* by Virgil Elizondo
- *Listening to God's Word* by Alice Camille
- *Community* by Adela Gonzalez
- *Incarnation* by John Shea
- And many others.

To learn more about forthcoming titles in the series, go to *orbisbooks.com*.

To learn more about resources for total parish catechesis, including children's materials that cover the same topics as *Catholic Spirituality for Adults,* please visit rclbenziger.com.

Please support your local bookstore.

Thank you for reading *Prayer* by Joyce Rupp. We hope you found it beneficial.